A YEAR IN YOUR GARDEN

David Tarrant

A YEAR IN YOUR GARDEN

A MONTH-BY-MONTH GUIDE
TO GARDENING IN BRITISH COLUMBIA

Whitecap Books
Vancouver/Toronto

Edited by Elaine Jones
Cover Photograph by Derik Murray
Cover design by Brad Nickason
Interior design by Bob English

Second printing 1989
Third printing 1991
Fourth printing 1995

Typeset at The Typeworks, Vancouver

Printed and bound in Canada by Friesen Printers, Altona, Manitoba

Canadian Cataloguing in Publication Data
Tarrant, David
    A year in your garden

    Includes index.
    ISBN 0-921061-27-7

    1. Gardening.   I. Title.
55453.T37 1989 635 C89-091035-9

CONTENTS

Acknowledgments
Preface

January   1

The New Year for Gardeners   1
Planning Your Garden   2
Terrariums and Bottle Gardens   5
The Winter Garden in Flower   7
New Pots for Houseplants   9
Houseplant and Bulb Maintenance   12
Winter Gardening and Clean-up   14

February   18

Planting Trees and Shrubs   18
Preparation for Spring   21
Time to Get the Fuchsias Out   22
Pruning Roses   24
Houseplants from Cuttings   26
Gardening for Everyone   29

March   31

Perennials—Flowers Year after Year   31
Seed Sowing   34
Peas and Broad Beans   36
Herbs for Your Garden   38
Planting Roses   40

April   42

Transplanting Seedlings   42
Planning a Fruit Garden   44

CONTENTS

Spring Pruning of Flowering Trees and Shrubs 47
Planning a Cut Flower Border 49
Hanging Baskets 52
Bedding Plants 54

May 57

Planting-out and Sowing Time 57
Spring and Summer Bulbs 59
Balcony and Patio Gardens 61
Vegetable Gardens—Planting out Warm Crops 63
Planting for Colour 66
Lawns and Ground Covers 68
Bugs and Pests 72
Fungus Diseases 74

June 77

Water Gardens 77
Weed, Feed, and Water 79
Between Seasons 81
Putting Houseplants out for the Summer 84
Rose Care 86

July 88

The Vegetable Patch—Replacement Vegetables 88
Cool Wet Weather 90
Houseplants in Summer 92
Summer Propogation—Growing Your Own Shrubs 94
Trimming Evergreens 96

August 99

Preserving Summer's Colours 99
Flowers from Cuttings and Seeds 102
Late Summer Sun and Summer Maintenance 104

September 107

Making Summer Last 107
Garden Evaluation 109
September Tidy-up 111
Cold Frames and Greenhouses 112
Indoor Gardens 114
Bulbs for Spring 116
Winter Planters 118

October 120

Flowers for Christmas 120
Putting the Garden to Bed 123
Harvesting and Storing Vegetables 126
Composting 128
Fall Care of Houseplants 131
Fall Colour 133

November 136

Winter Digging and Clean-up 136
Dormancy and Pruning 138
Growing Herbs and Greens under Lights 141
Your Garden in Winter 143
Winter Watch 145

December 148

Planting up Your Own Gifts 148
Gifts for Gardeners 150
Christmas Trees and Such 153
Caring for Christmas Gift Plants 155

Index 157

ACKNOWLEDGMENTS

First of all, I'd like to thank *The Vancouver Sun* for giving me the opportunity to write the weekly columns that form the basis of this book. I'd also like to acknowledge UBC Botanical Garden for affording me the opportunity to work in a stimulating environment, where I can do what I most like to do and where I can both learn and help others. Seane Trehearne at the UBC Plant Science Greenhouse kindly provided the setting and assistance for the cover photograph. Finally, a thank-you to editor Elaine Jones, for her diligence in pulling this all together in book form.

PREFACE

General gardening books are always difficult to write, and this one certainly isn't meant to cover all bases.

However, for the beginning gardener in British Columbia, it gives some guidelines for a year in your garden, following a month-by-month pattern. Of course, the monthly planning will have to be adapted by each reader for his or her own area, as climate varies so much throughout the province, and you will find suggestions for this throughout the book.

The contents are drawn from my weekly columns in *The Vancouver Sun* over the past several years. The columns lend themselves to the monthly format, and they have been revised and updated to keep them abreast of current information. I hope that having them in this form will be useful—both to those who already follow my column and to new readers.

Use this book in a general way to help frame up your year in the garden, and as a means of generating ideas, but remember that it is not a comprehensive guide to gardening in the Pacific region. You will probably want to use it along with books that give more detailed information on many of the subjects touched on here.

As you make your way through the months in this little book, enjoy. Then branch out on your own and experiment. Above all, keep a logbook about your own garden on a regular basis.

I hope you will find this book easy to read and perhaps a little amusing from time to time. I feel extremely fortunate to be working in a field that I consider to be my hobby, but I strongly believe that gardening should be fun for everyone—not just a chore that you have to do, but a place to escape from the everyday routines of life. Happy gardening!

J A N U A R Y

CHAPTER ONE

The New Year for Gardeners

Part of the fun of gardening is to sit back with a cup of coffee or tea and a bundle of seed catalogues and plan for the season ahead. Local garden centres won't be stocking their shelves with new seed for some weeks to come, and while the selection they carry has broadened over the last few years, it is still fun to order something different from a seed catalogue.

At this time of year the new catalogues come out, and each year it seems there are more and more to choose from. Dominion Seed House, Georgetown, Ontario, L7G 4A2, and Stokes Seeds, 39 James Street, Box 10, Ontario, L2R 6R6, are both free and have a wide selection of seeds and other garden accessories to choose from. McFayden Seed Company, PO Box 1800, Brandon, Manitoba, R7A 6N4, is particularly good for interior and northern B.C. gardeners as they carry hardy prairie roses, trees, shrubs, and many varieties of vegetables suitable for the shorter season. Territorial Seed Company, Box 1200, 133 West 5th Avenue, Vancouver, B.C., V5Y 3X1, specializes in varieties most suitable for our climate, and carry a lot of the older favourites which are sometimes hard to find. The last two mentioned cost a dollar, so send it along with your request.

Both of these are available through Thompson and Morgan, and if ordered in January will arrive in time to sow for beautiful hanging baskets in the summer.

Now is also the time to check out your supplies of leftover seeds from last season. The best place to keep spare seed is in the crisper drawer of your refrigerator in an airtight container, such as a plastic food container. Seed that is stored at a constant cool temperature is good for years, and all the major botanical gardens of the world run their seed banks this way.

If you've been gardening for a year or more, your own records will be an invaluable part of planning each year's garden. By keeping records you can know which crops or flowers did well, which failed to prosper, and how to rotate your crops. Record everything—sowing dates, weather, how long crops take to develop, whether the crop did poorly and why. The longer you have kept records the more valuable they will be, as success or failure of certain crops depends a great deal on the weather and with each year you increase your information on the weather and how it affects your garden.

After keeping records for a year or two, your logbook will become your very own practical gardening guide that applies specifically to your own area–better than anything you can buy.

Now that you have your seed catalogues and logbook at hand, you can start planning the garden you want for this coming season. No matter how many years you have been gardening, it is still fun to dream over seed catalogues and order some new seed. The pleasure derived from growing them will be endless.

Planning
Your Garden

You don't have to be a landscape architect to draw up a plan of your garden, and you'll find it very useful for planning what you want to plant this coming season. This is particularly important for the vegetable patch, so that you can organize crop rotation. If you grow the same crop in the same place year after year, that crop will take specific nutrients from the soil, eventually depleting it. Crop rotation is also good practice because of disease, as some fungus diseases that attack roots overwinter in the soil, just waiting to re-infect the same crop the next year.

Where you had root vegetables last year, plant peas or beans, or any of the cabbage or lettuce group. Root crops use up a lot of phosphate, whereas lettuce, spinach and cabbage take more nitrogen from the soil. Members of the legume family–peas and beans–are very clever, as they manufacture their own nitrogen in nodules on their root system. If you cut them back when they have finished producing, and then dig the roots in, they replenish the nitrogen content of your soil. This coming year, plant the cabbages where the peas were, the peas where the beets were, and the beets where the cabbages were.

If you've been gardening for some years, you probably have your favourite vegetables, but if you want to experiment, here are some suggestions for vegetables that have worked well. A new 'Sweet 100' type of tomato, 'Chelsea', tolerated the heat of a southwest-facing balcony in a 30-centimetre (12-inch) pot, and produced an abundance of fruit despite the fact that the plant dried out now and then. 'Early Cascade' is another good choice. Grown in a half-barrel on a hot, southwest-facing deck, it bore thin-skinned, medium-sized tomatoes.

Amongst the peas, 'Novella' is one of the so-called leafless peas and is excellent for the small home garden, reaching an overall height of 30 to 40 centimetres (12 to 16 inches) and producing an abundance of delicious peas. Peas are sometimes difficult to get started, but a product that really works is Nature's Aid. It puts millions of live nitrogen-fixing 3 bacteria into the soil when it's sprinkled along the rows, assuring good germination. Potatoes are fun and easy to grow even for a first-time gardener. I still find 'Early Warba' hard to beat for early new potatoes. And you might try a vegetable spaghetti squash this year; they are delicious and a pleasant change from the glut of zucchinis that we all experience each year.

A new cabbage sprout called 'Ormavon F1' produced good firm brussels sprouts right to the top, and, as promised, a tender cabbage at the top of each plant. The nice thing about it is the cabbage can be harvested without harming the sprout crop.

You can also plan your annual flower display in the same way by making a rough map of your flower garden. This is the time of year to plan, when you can work out such fine points as blooming time, complementary colours and heights of each variety. Some seed catalogues give the heights, but if they don't, there is no better time to visit your library and borrow some volumes on the great gardens and gardeners of the world.

Among the new varieties of flowers available are a hibiscus, 'Disco Belles Mixed.' They are the closest thing I have seen to those gorgeous tropical hibiscus that one sees in Hawaii, and they can be grown from seed. The plants reach about 45 centimetres (18 inches) in height and bear enormous flowers up to 23 centimetres (9 inches) across, ranging in colour from white to dark red. But they need a good, hot, sunny spot to do well in B.C. gardens.

If you are a poppy lover like me, then an annual called 'Dandbrog' is a must. It has blood-red blooms which have a white blotch at the base, giving a cross effect, and the edges of the petals are daintily laced or fringed. Nemesia is another favourite and it is easy to grow. The seed companies have come out with a mixture called 'Tapestry', which includes many blue and purple shades among the more familiar yellows, reds, and oranges.

A point to remember when planning is to note not only colour, but perfume. This was brought home to me one warm summer, when the evening scent of the garden was a joy. For a beautifully scented evening garden, grow nicotiana, or flowering tobacco. The good old-fashioned white is still the most highly scented of them all. If you have a really good hot spot, try heliotrope (or, as we always called it, cherry pie, as that is what it smells like). However, be warned, it isn't easy to grow from seed, so it might be best to purchase bedding plants later on in May.

There are other sweet-smelling flowers that aren't as showy, but worth garden space. One is the old night-scented stock, listed as matthiola. Another is mignonette. You wouldn't give either a second look, but the overpowering perfume will certainly turn your head.

So you see there is much to think about and plan at this otherwise dreary time of year. And on those brighter days go out and take a good look at your garden. If there are trees and shrubs that are overcrowding other plants, give some thought to either moving them or completely getting rid of them. Tag the ones to be moved, as next month is a good time to tackle that chore.

Terrariums and Bottle Gardens

After the fun and excitement of the holidays, January can often seem dull, especially for gardeners. This slow time is a perfect opportunity to make a terrarium. I know they are somewhat old-fashioned, but believe me, they are fun to create. Terrariums can be created in an old pickle jar, an unused aquarium, or a large cider or wine jug left over from the holidays. As long as it is clear glass, it will make a fascinating garden.

Making a garden in a bottle requires some special techniques. Because the neck of the bottle is small, you will need to make some tools. Have ready two strong bamboo canes, such as those used for staking in the garden, some strong masking tape or scotch tape, a cork small

5

enough to get through the neck of the bottle, and a small teaspoon.

Make the canes about 45 centimetres (18 inches) long. Sharpen one cane and jab it firmly into the cork. As an extra precaution, fasten the cork securely to the cane with masking tape (I have lost many corks inside the bottle).

Next, attach the teaspoon to the second cane by binding the handle to the cane with tape. Assemble your potting mix, gravel, charcoal, and plants. You will need a funnel to get all this into the bottle, and you can make one very easily by cutting the end off a plastic container, such as a dishwashing detergent bottle. The pouring end makes the funnel spout.

At the very base of the bottle, place a layer of pea gravel. This will allow drainage of excess moisture. Any gravel is fine, but if you collect it outside, pour some boiling water over it to sterilize it before using.

Depending on the depth and size of your bottle, make the gravel 1 ½ to 2 centimetres (¾ to 1 inch) deep. As you drop it through the funnel, it will form a mountain on the bottom, which you can then level out with the cork tool. On top of that, place a fine layer of charcoal, available from any garden centre. A bottle garden is capped, and could turn sour quite quickly without a layer of charcoal to help keep the excess water at the base of the bottle sweet.

The soil can be any good sterilized potting mix. I don't recommend adding fertilizer when making a bottle garden, as the humidity will be so high that the plants will grow quite fast enough. I do like to mix a handful of charcoal into the potting mix, though.

Moisten the mix before you add it to the jar. It should be just wet enough to stick together when squeezed lightly in the palm of your hand. Because it is moist, you will need to help it through the funnel with the cane end of one of your tools. Level it off with the cork tool.

Don't get carried away when adding the soil; about 5 centimetres (2 inches) is ample. Check the level frequently.

For a bottle garden, use very small plants, the smallest you can find at your plant shop or garden center. Three or four are the maximum number in such a tiny garden. Some good choices might be selaginella (sweat moss), fittonia (nerve plant), helxine (babies' tears), and perhaps pilea (creeping charlie). All these are fairly slow-growing and used to poorer light conditions as they are native to jungle floors.

Wash the soil from their roots, and cover them with moist paper towel until the bottle is ready. To plant, tilt the bottle slightly and dig a hole with the spoon. With the bottle still tilted, drop in your first plant so that it has most of its roots in the hole. Use the teaspoon to cover the roots with soil and firm it in place with the cork.

When you have finished all your planting, puff a few sprays of moisture in from your plant mister, to clean the neck of the bottle, and leave the jar in good light (but not direct sun) with the cork off for a day or two. Then put the lid on and if a build-up of moisture occurs on the inside of the glass and stays for half a day, take the top off again. It will be ready to be sealed when the condensation on the glass stays within a few centimetres (1 inch) of the potting surface.

Place your bottle garden near a table lamp or other light source. The plants will be very happy giving off carbon dioxide at night and recycling it as oxygen during the day and all you'll need to do is watch it grow as it waters itself.

The Winter Garden in Flower

Although winter has a firm hold on the interior of B.C. in January, those living on the coast can grow many lovely winter flowering plants in home gardens at this time of year. And while this isn't necessarily the time to plant them, it is a good time to make a note of those you like, so that when spring planting time comes along, you will be able to make room for one or two plants in your garden.

The majority of small trees and shrubs that bloom at this time, such as winter jasmine, winter cherry, and viburnum, have their origins in Asia. The botanical name of winter jasmine is *Jasminum nudiflorum,* 7 which means that it flowers when there are no leaves on the stems. And while it doesn't have the perfume of its many sub-tropical relatives, it is really eye-catching on mild winter days, when it's covered with little yellow trumpet flowers, not unlike forsythia.

Winter jasmine, which is often treated as a climber in home gardens, needs help to climb–such as frequent tying-in to a trellis or some other support system. I have also seen it used quite effectively on banks, as a ground cover, and it works well tumbling out of large window boxes or roof planters. When planting jasmine, choose a sheltered west- or south-facing site and work well-rotted compost or leaf-mould into the top 30 centimetres (12 inches) of soil.

The winter cherry should really be called the autumn cherry, as its botanical name is *Prunus subhertella autumnalis* and autumn is the normal time of the year for it to bloom. You see it used quite widely as a street tree and it can be quite a traffic-stopper for visitors or new residents in B.C. A good small tree for a home garden, it is no taller than 6 metres (20 feet) at maturity. The fall foliage is usually a good colour and the flowers start to bloom in early November, right after leaf drop. They start out white and as they mature they blush pink.

If you are considering a winter cherry for your garden, perhaps as a single specimen tree in the lawn, try to choose a site which is easily seen from your livingroom or kitchen window. This way you'll enjoy the flowers during the grey days of winter without having to go outside.

The winter variety of viburnum, *Viburnum farreri*, is another great shrub for the winter garden. Viburnum forms a shrub no more than 3 metres (10 feet) in height. As soon as the leaves drop, the flowers start to appear in clusters, which are quite pink in the bud stage and eventually become pale pink in full bloom. The scent is delicious, and a small branch cut and put in a vase in a warm room will perfume the whole living area. In fact, I would say that if you only had room for one winter flowering plant in your garden, this would have to be it. My mentor in England, Frances Perry, has a hedge along the south side of her garden, which is from the original seed collection of Reginald Farrer, brought from China in the early 1900s.

Those in the interior who have a large glassed-in heated porch, or a large picture window facing south, could try growing another heavily scented winter jasmine, *J. polyanthum*, which usually blooms in November. It tends to ramble or climb, and will even work well in a large hanging pot. The flowers are in clusters and the petals are pure white on the inside, pink to darkish red on the outside. It was a favourite in the old conservatories in England, but some of you might find the scent a little overpowering. The secret of success with this plant is moderate temperatures, around 17°C (64°F) by day and as cool as 10° (50°F) at night.

If you don't have access to a garden and are longing to see a little greenery, take along a pair of pruners when you go out for a walk in the bush. Cut branches of such native shrubs as willow, hazelnut, and thimbleberry, put them in a vase in a warm room, and sit back and watch them open over the coming weeks.

Of course, there are houseplants that you can enjoy at this time, as well. Among them is cyclamen, that exotic marble-leafed plant whose flowers have their beautiful petals turned back as though they were falling gently through the air. Cyclamen, which grows from a corm, loves cooler temperatures, particularly at night. Try to keep it in good light during the day and in a cooler, but frost-free, place at night.

New Pots
for Houseplants

Very soon your houseplants will begin responding to the ever-so-slightly lengthening days by beginning to put on new growth. Just prior to this new growth, feeder roots will start developing in the pot, so anytime between now and February is a good time to repot.

You should know, however, that there are some plants that resent being repotted. As a general rule, hoya, Christmas cactus and related cactus (such as Thanksgiving), clivia, and perhaps some of the cym-bidium orchids bloom best when pot-bound. Repotting won't hurt them, but it will stop them from flowering for the next two to three years. Cymbidium orchids do need repotting every three years or so, but timing is critical and it should be immediately after they have fin-ished flowering.

Apart from these exceptions, all your plants would enjoy a fresh layer of potting mix, which is exactly what repotting means. It doesn't mean taking plants from one pot and shaking or washing all the soil off the roots and giving them totally new soil.

First of all, select a pot that is just 3 to 5 centimetres (1 ¼ to 2 inches) larger than the one your plant is in. Never repot to a too-large pot, as plants like their feeder roots near the outer edge of the pot, where there is a good supply of air and moisture. If there is a large amount of pot-ting mix, the roots never make it to the edge of the pot, causing a slow-down in growth. Most plants should be repotted annually until they reach a pot size of 45 centimetres (18 inches). At that point they will be too large to repot, but they can be kept going for a number of years with regular feeding and an annual application of fresh potting mix to the surface.

Next, get some good, all-purpose tropical potting mix from your local garden centre. Peat, which is basically a sterile medium, is the basis for all pre-packaged potting mixes. It is consistent in its content, as op-posed to soil, which varies from area to area and has a broad and vari-able range of mineral nutrients. You can make your own soil mix using garden soil, but it is important to sterilize it before using it for houseplants. If you don't, you will have problems with weeds germinat-ing, fungus in the soil, and other diseases. (See page 42 for instructions on mixing and treating homemade soil mix.)

Most potting mixes do not have any fertilizer added to them unless it is stated on the bag, so you will need to add some yourself. My all-round, standard favourite is granular 6-8-6 all-purpose fertilizer, which I add at the rate of 15 millilitres (1 tablespoon) to a level household pail of potting mix. Thoroughly blend it through the whole pail and moisten it well before using. Most potting media are 90 percent peat and if they are dry in the bag, they're difficult to moisten. The secret here is to use hot water when moistening the mix.

The plants themselves should be well-watered before repotting. Water the night before or at least two hours ahead, so that the whole root mass is moist.

To get the plant out of its pot, put your hand across the top of the pot so that the plant's stem is between your middle two fingers. Then turn the whole thing upside-down and sharply tap the rim of the pot on a wooden surface. If the plant has been well watered it should slide out with ease and sit on your hand like a sand castle.

Now you can observe the roots. If they cover 50 percent or more of the exposed surface, then the plant definitely needs repotting. (Be careful not to break up the roots; if the feeder roots are disturbed it will cause yellowing and leaf drop.) If the roots cover less than 50 percent of the surface, then the original pot should be slipped back on and the plant left for another year.

Assuming it is ready, put a little drainage material over the hole in the bottom of the new pot (broken up styrofoam cups or crumpled-up plastic pots will do) and add a handful of fresh potting mix. Then put the plant in place and check the original soil level against the rim of the pot. There should be several centimetres (1 inch) between the rim of the pot and the surface of the soil level for ease of watering. If the plant isn't in the right position, you may have to lift it out and add more soil.

Once the level is right, fill in the gap with fresh mix, lightly tapping the pot on the table as you go, to settle the soil well. You can use your fingers to tamp the soil down, or if the gap is too small, use a pencil to firm it.

Once finished, level it off and water to further settle the soil mix. Stand the plant in an area where you can keep an eye on it for the first week or so, by which time it will be settled in and have new nourishment for the soon-to-be-produced new roots.

Houseplant and Bulb Maintenance

The end of January is not only the time to repot houseplants, but to think about general maintenance of bulbs that were forced to bloom earlier this month and the pruning of larger plants like hibiscus, bougainvillea, and gardenia.

Once amaryllis bulbs have finished blooming, cut off just the flower heads, leaving the long bare stem. Keep the plant in the best light possible to encourage good strong leaf development and feed it every ten days with a weak solution of liquid plant food. If the label suggests 5 millilitres (1 teaspoon) for each three litres (quarts) of water, then dilute it to half that strength.

During the next three months the development of leaf growth is very important, as the bulb builds up its flower for next season. I know a lot of you have great difficulty encouraging your amaryllis to die back naturally in April when the leaves look their healthiest, but this is important—these plants are native to South Africa where they are used to suddenly drying up in the heat of summer and literally baking in the sun. You must gradually reduce the amount of water you give the bulb, and once the leaves have died back, the pot should be placed on its side in a sunny spot, such as a shelf in a greenhouse or sun porch. In the fall, take the bulb from its pot, get rid of all the old soil, and repot into some good potting mix with fertilizer added. I guarantee it will bloom well again next year.

Similarly, with other bulbs that have been forced, such as hyacinths and narcissi, it is important to let their leaves grow for a couple of months or so. However, they will not be suitable for forcing again next year and paperwhite narcissi won't be any use at all after one season's growth, as they aren't hardy. But others can be kept growing, and if they don't look too pretty, hide them among other plants or put them in the best light in your basement. As soon as the weather warms up, plant them out into your garden, where they will die down naturally and return as regular spring bulbs next year.

While on the subject of bulbs, if you were caught by surprise with early winter weather and still haven't planted all your spring bulbs in the garden, keep your unplanted bulbs in a cool, frost-free, dry area and plant them as early in the spring as possible. (Those who live in coastal areas will be able to plant them any time now.) I can just hear some gardeners muttering words of dismay at such a suggestion, as it is terribly unorthodox, but bulbs have to be planted some time before next summer, otherwise they'll be no good at all.

This is the best time of year to prune your indoor hibiscus. In fact, older plants will benefit greatly from quite a severe pruning (by that I mean cutting back into older hard wood). As with all pruning, make the cut just above an outward-facing bud. On older hibiscus, such buds may be difficult to detect, but if you look really closely, you'll see little horizontal lines that go half-way around the stem at regular intervals. These are old leaf scars that have dormant growth buds just above them in the middle of the line.

Don't worry about cutting it back too much—you can reduce the overall height of the plant by two-thirds. It sounds drastic, I know, but your plant will love you for it. Sometimes after such hard pruning, the older wood takes longer to shoot out, but if you place it in a high-humidity area, like the bathroom or kitchen, the moisture will make it bud faster.

Bougainvillea can also benefit from drastic pruning at this time; the same rule of cutting back by two-thirds applies. But be careful of the thorns; they're quite vicious. For both these plants, once new growth begins to show, feed them about every ten days with a plant food similar to 20-20-20.

Winter Gardening and Clean-up

Even if you have snow in your garden, this is a good time of year to get your berry bushes pruned. Most of the bush and berry fruits originate in nature from the edge of deciduous woods or forests. There the soil is rich and the bushes receive a nice top dressing of organic material each fall as the leaves drop. Pruning doesn't occur in nature, unless there is a fire or other natural occurrence, but we prune berry bushes in our gardens to produce the best quality fruit.

Raspberries form the best fruit on the younger wood that was produced last season and hasn't yet borne fruit. The first thing to do is to cut out all the pale beige canes that produced fruit last year. Prune them out as close to the ground as possible. Next select the strongest of the brighter orange-brown shoots, and tie them in to your support wires, about 15 centimetres (6 inches) apart. If your top support is 2 metres (6 feet) from ground level, any canes higher than that should be reduced to a uniform height three or four buds above the wire. Cut out any excess or spindly shoots that are left, as they will only rob the good canes of nourishment and if left, they would produce poor fruit.

If you have the fall-bearing raspberries that produce delicious berries from September until frost, cut all the canes back to the ground now. All the strong growth sent up in the coming summer will bear fruit.

Red and white currants are a different story, as they fruit best on two- or three-year-old wood. If yours are old bushes, then one or two of the oldest branches can be taken out as close to soil level as possible and any crossing branches or ones that are growing into the centre of the bush can be cut back lightly. Basically, it is the same pruning that is carried out on gooseberries.

Gooseberries are not widely grown but they deserve to be. They produce excellent berries for gooseberry pie, and if left on the bush until they are really ripe, they are deliciously sweet to eat out of your hand. Maybe they don't enjoy as much popularity as they should because of their thorns, but with proper pruning at this time you can make enough room between the branches to get your hand in to pick the fruit, as well as letting as much sunlight as possible in to ripen the berries.

This job is much like pruning a larger fruit tree. First remove any dead wood or crossing branches, and any branches that are too low to the ground. Gooseberries have that habit of sending out branches right at ground level, and while these branches look strong and healthy, with lots of fruit buds, they should be the first branches to be removed. Any fruit developing on them will be on the ground and full of slugs and other insect pests.

Once all the branches already mentioned are gone, you will have a much better overall picture of the bush. At this stage, you should reduce each branch leader shoot by about one-third, cutting just above an outward-facing bud. Then prune back the spurs, or side shoots, that grow all the way down each branch to two or three buds. These are the fruiting spurs and each of them should produce fruit.

Blackberries and related crops like loganberries and tayberries will produce large juicy fruits on the long runners that grew all over your garden last summer. For this job, get your gloves on and prune away all the growth that was tied in last season. Next select six to eight of the longest runners and tie them onto your wires in pairs or groups of three, depending on how many support wires you have available. The excess runners should be cut out.

While these latter crops are somewhat ungainly to grow in a small home garden, don't overlook them as possible vines for screening off your patio. They make quick seasonal screens that produce delicious fruit.

Blueberries that are less than six years old generally do not require pruning, as they are slow-growing compared to blackberries. Usually blueberries produce many little fruiting spurs that will bear good fruit for up to five years. After that the bushes are maintained with renewal pruning.

When doing renewal pruning, take a good look at the bush to determine where the oldest branches are. They will show up as darker wood that has tended to form bark much like that on a larger tree. Remove one or perhaps two of these old branches as close to the ground as pos- 15 sible. This will encourage new growth that will produce good fruit a couple of years hence. It's always a bit of a problem to remove the old branches, but that is where one of those curve-bladed pruning saws or a pair of long-handled pruners comes in very handy.

Once you have done all this pruning, spray your bushes and fruit trees with dormant oil spray to take care of such problems as scale and overwintering insect eggs. You should also spray with lime sulphur, which is terribly stinky stuff that smells like rotten eggs, but it is the best remedy for killing fungus spores. When using either of these products, always wear protective clothing and a mask. Only spray on a still, frost-free, dry day, so that the sprays have a chance to dry on the branches before nightfall. If you have experienced problems with fungus diseases, spray the ground around the base of the bushes, out to the drip line. This will kill any overwintering spores that may be there.

If there are any large perennial weeds that have survived the winter, carefully remove them without disturbing the soil too much. Whatever you do, don't dig among berry bushes as they are all surface-rooted, and you'll just expose and damage the roots, doing more harm than good.

To finish off, top dress or mulch each of your berry bushes with a layer of well-rotted compost or manure to a depth of 5 centimetres (2 inches) all over the root area. It will simulate that natural top dressing they get in the bush, prevent drying out, and will help produce delicious fruit.

If you get too cold out in the garden, doing all that, you can go into a warmer place like the basement and take a good look at all your gardening tools. Now is a great time to clean them up. Of course, really good gardeners clean their tools every time they put them away, but if you are like me you are not as thorough. First get some good, warm soapy water and wash off all the spades, forks, shovels, and trowels. If they have rust spots, scrub them with some steel wool. Once they are clean and dry, polish them with an oily rag to protect them against rust.

Treat pruning shears the same way, although it is important with pruning blades that they always be cleaned immediately after pruning one bush and before going to the next. This is necessary to prevent the spread of diseases such as black knot, bacterial canker on plums, and canker on apple trees.

While you are cleaning the tools, give the special area or shed where you keep them a good clean too. You'll be surprised what turns up— you could find the gardening gloves you've been missing all year! Finally, take your garden shears and mower blades to be professionally sharpened. Now you are all ready for the season ahead.

FEBRUARY

CHAPTER TWO

Planting
Trees and Shrubs

In the warmer areas of our province we have a wealth of beautiful trees and shrubs to choose from for our gardens. Whether you are starting a garden from scratch or have an established garden that needs a bit of thinning out and replanting, if you live on the coast the month of February is the time to plant or move trees and shrubs (those in the interior should wait until March). The principles are the same for both new and older gardens.

First of all, it is most important to know the overall potential height at maturity of the plant you are considering, to ensure that the space is large enough. Quite often nursery labels don't provide this information, but libraries are excellent places to research all aspects of gardens.

The other thing to consider is the light factor. Don't underestimate the influence of tall trees or buildings. I have seen young apple trees that were planted 10 metres (33 feet) away from large cedar trees in what seemed to be an open space, and they still grew all their new branches facing away from the large trees. This might be something you have to live with in your garden, but make sure that the tree or shrub you have chosen for the site has enough light for its needs.

For example, many people think rhododendrons need shade, but most varieties don't tolerate complete shade well. They should get at least a half-day of sun for the flower buds to develop and ripen.

Also be aware of the hardiness of the plant. Even in the mild coastal areas, some shrubs or trees must be protected from northern and eastern winds. Similarly, take care not to plant in a low part of the garden where winter frost can linger through the day. Low spots also tend to be wet, and there are few plants that like to grow where their roots are in puddles all winter long.

If you are dealing with a new garden, be warned: there is a terrible tendency to overplant. You may think that the garden will look empty, or you might want instant privacy. But if you are fully aware that you are overplanting for instant effect, make sure you put three or more of your desired trees or shrubs together, so that later on, three to five years down the road, two of them can be removed easily without ruining the overall effect.

Remember too that overplanting is costly. A better approach might be to space correctly, filling in with annuals and bulbs for the first few years.

New trees and shrubs will either be in large nursery pot containers or bare root with a fairly sizeable root ball. Dig the hole twice the width and about half a spade deeper than the size of the root ball, if possible. Next mix some well-rotted compost or manure and a handful of superphosphate into the bottom of the hole. Then set your new tree or shrub in place and check to see that it will be at the same level it was in its container or previous home. Never bury them deeper than they were originally—a general rule of thumb for all replanting and potting.

Fill in the gap around the root area with some soil that has compost and superphosphate mixed through it, firming it in with your foot as you go. Stand back from time to time to make sure it is straight. Even if the soil is already moist, water it in, and make a note to yourself to give newly planted trees and shrubs extra water during any dry spells for the whole year ahead.

Staking is important for trees. For larger trees, the stake is often placed in the hole before the soil is filled back in. When tying the trunk   19 to the stake, do not tie it tight; leave plenty of room for growth. There are excellent rubber ties available at garden centres just for this purpose.

Shrubs such as rhododendrons, azaleas and camellias are easy to move as they have good fibrous root systems, but deciduous shrubs like forsythia and ornamental Japanese quince are not as easy. Moving any shrubs in the pre-spring period means sacrificing the flowers for a year, and in the case of rhodendrons and camellias all the flower buds should be taken off prior to moving the plant. I know it will break your heart to do it, but if left on they'll drain a lot of the plant's energy, perhaps to the point of killing it. Deciduous shrubs lose a lot of soil when being lifted as a result of their open root system, so all the top growth should be pruned back to within 30 centimetres (12 inches) of the soil level. This will promote good root and shoot growth through the coming season.

While we're on the subject of replanting, if you're reworking your garden, you may want to move some of your perennials. They include such plants as delphiniums, asters (commonly called Michaelmas daisies), and peonies. All perennials like deeply worked soil with plenty of well-rotted manure or compost worked in. The best time for moving them is when the new growth starts to show, and this can be any time between now and March or April. For directions on moving well-established perennials, see page 31.

For all planting and moving, the best days are those dull grey ones just prior to rain. Don't do it if the soil is very wet, as the compaction caused when you firm the soil will restrict future growth. You want a dull day so that roots that are exposed to the air do not dry out. Any plant that has to be out of the ground for longer than ten minutes or so should always have its roots wrapped in plastic or some damp burlap.

Preparation for Spring

The official beginning of spring is still some weeks away, but a mild February can be very spring-like. Don't get carried away with seed sowing yet, however—planting-out time is a long time away. It can be a little earlier for those on the coast, but as a general guideline, I would say that the third week of May is quite early enough for most areas. And three months is far too long to keep seedlings inside.

There are things you should be doing soon in readiness for spring. If you haven't dug over your vegetable garden, now is a good time for it, provided your garden is free of snow. One of the advantages of digging at this time of year is that many of the hardier weeds have started to germinate already and by disturbing them at this time it will prevent them from taking over.

The main difference between fall and spring digging is in the type of manure that is added to the soil. At this time of the year only old manure should be used. By that I mean manure that has been piled up over the winter so that it has decomposed a bit and the winter rains have had a chance to wash out harmful burning salts. The most dangerous manures are chicken and turkey, which can really burn. However, if they are available at this time, they can be composted for use later on. Compost can be added at any time as it will be well rotted.

One of the questions asked most frequently by first-year gardeners is how much manure or organic matter to apply. With few exceptions, most vegetables have their roots in the top 30 centimetres (12 inches) of soil only, so dig to a spade's depth and add a shovelful of manure for each spade's width. It is also important that the manure is well buried so that it encourages the roots to go down into the ground. Manure left near the surface encourages roots to stay at the surface, where they will suffer if there is a dry summer.

Once your garden is dug, lime can be added. Of the various types of lime available, the more expensive dolomite lime is the best, as it will be available longer in your soil. If you can't get dolomite, regular agricultural lime will do. Apply it at a good handful per square metre (square yard) so that there is an even dusting over the whole surface. 21

For those of you that are looking for an easier way to grow vegetables, you may consider putting in some raised beds at this time. Instructions for making these beds are on page 29. Raised beds can be as high as you require them, so that you can sit or stand and work at them comfortably. If you've never tried raised bed gardening you might be surprised at the results—the soil warms up much earlier, resulting in earlier crops.

If you covered any perennials with leaves in the fall for winter protection, they can probably be removed some time around now, depending on your location and the weather. Spread the leaves around the plant as a mulch; they will rot down and provide good nourishing humus. Finally, since spent mushroom manure is available at this time of the year, get a load and top dress any shrubs or fruit bushes to a depth of 10 centimetres (4 inches).

Time to Get the Fuchsias out

When the sun gets warmer I know gardeners start to get enthused about sowing seeds for spring, even though it's too early. But one of the things you can do at this time of year is to get out those overwintered fuchsias, geraniums and marguerites.

If you buried them underground last fall, open up the trench carefully and separate the plants. I hope the permanent marker pen has stayed on the labels so that you can tell the different varieties; if not, you'll just have to wait for them to bloom. After lifting them, plant each one individually into the smallest-sized pot it will fit into—perhaps the 15-centimetre (6-inch) ones. Depending on how sheltered the location and how warm it has been, some of the plants may have started to send out spindly white shoots. Remove all these shoots, pruning them back to just above the lower dormant buds. If there are no new shoots, prune the roots back to fill the smallest pot.

Next, pot them in some good potting mix that has some fertilizer thoroughly mixed through before using—something like granular 6-8-6 at 15 millilitres (1 tablespoon) per household pailful of potting mix. Drainage material is seldom put into the bottom of smaller pots these days, but I use a paper towel to cover the drainage holes. It stops the soil from pouring out each time I water. Remember to leave a few centimetres (1 inch) between the surface of the soil and the rim of the pot for watering later on.

If there aren't any shoots showing yet, don't worry about pruning the tops. After potting place the pots on a sunny window ledge, in a greenhouse, or under grow-lights. If they have overwintered well, the shoots will start to become visible after a very few days. At that time, prune back to just above them. Fuchsias are usually the first to sprout, followed closely by geraniums. The marguerites tend to take longer.

The plants will do fine in this location until about the end of March. Then they should be potted on into larger pots or hanging baskets, and put into a cold frame or cool greenhouse until mid-May, when it should be safe to put them outside.

Use the same treatment for any plants that may have been overwintered in boxes in the basement or crawl-space. However, if you have kept these plants growing over the winter in a heated greenhouse or sun room, now is the time to prune them back, as chances are the winter growth has been rather straggly. If you don't prune, the new growth which is now beginning to look good near the top will develop further, leaving the middle of the plant leafless and unattractive later in the summer. As a general guideline, cut them back to within 15 centimetres (6 inches) of the soil level. Don't be afraid to prune them, even if it means losing healthy-looking growth; you can always use the cuttings for propagation.

If these plants are still in the original hanging baskets they were in all last summer, repot them into fresh potting mix, and put them back into the same basket.

I'm sure many of you have seen and coveted tree fuchsias for your patio. If you start now, with a little persistence you could have a good-looking fuchsia tree by midsummer. The secret is to start off with a good, strong, single-stemmed plant in a 10-centimetre (4-inch) pot. It should be staked, and while a greenhouse location would be nice, a good bright window in a house or apartment will do. In about six weeks the plant will need to be moved up to the next largest pot, a process that will continue all through the growing season. By fall the fuchsia will be about a metre (3 feet) in height and in a 30-centimetre (12-inch) pot.

As it grows, side shoots will appear at all the leaf axils. The secret is to leave these side shoots on, but don't let them grow any longer than two pairs of leaves each. Leaving them on strengthens the stem, and once the desired height is reached, they are pruned back flush with the stem. The shoots and branches at the top are left on to form the tree-like head.

Once fall arrives, growth will slow down considerably, but if you can keep the fuchsia in a house or greenhouse, you can continue to develop the branchwork. By the following season it will be a handsome fuchsia tree, probably in a 40-centimetre (16-inch) pot.

Pruning Roses

S ometimes February can be unseasonably warm, and when it is, those in coastal areas should check their roses. Often the uppermost buds are already unfolding tiny new leaves. As soon as the buds start to swell and turn pinkish red, it's time to prune.

Some readers will already know that I love to prune. It is a wonderful activity if you're feeling mad at the world, as you can snip away to your heart's content. When pruning regular old-fashioned hybrid tea roses, like 'Peace' or 'Crimson Glory', that drastic pruning is the best route to follow.

Many first-time pruners have a problem pruning the healthy new shoots that are well on the way at the top of the bush; they tend to take just a few centimetres (1 inch) from the end of each branch. But those top-growth buds are at the tips of branches that are probably a metre (3 feet) in height. Leaving that tip growth to develop will result in straggly growth that will shoot up another 60 centimetres (2 feet) or so. Your rose blooms will be well above eye level and the lower two-thirds of the bush won't develop any leaves—giving a very unsightly rosebush.

When pruning bush roses the guidelines are straightforward. First remove any dead wood, as close to the base of the bush as possible. Next take out all weak spindly growth from the centre of the bush and any branches that are crossing back across the middle. Lastly reduce the overall growth by two-thirds, making sure all cuts are above an outward-facing bud. If possible, make the cuts on an angle sloping back away from the bud. The buds down at the lower areas of the bush are not as easy to detect, but look for old leaf stem scars, which will appear as horizontal lines that curve one-third of the way around the stem. Just above the middle of each scar is a dormant bud. Even though these buds look very dormant compared to all those leafy advanced buds at the top, they will develop, producing good strong new growth from the base of the bush that will give the best roses you've ever had next June.

These same pruning techniques are true for most other types of bush roses, including polyantha and multiflora roses.

One thing to watch out for when pruning any roses is the disease known as crown gall. As the name suggests, it occurs down at the crown of the roots, just where the stems come from. It looks like a mass of greenish brown corky coral. If it is present, you should dig up and burn or destroy the whole bush. Unfortunately the disease stays in the soil for awhile, so you shouldn't plant another rose there for a year or two. If you have already pruned the bush before noticing the galls, wash your pruner blades thoroughly in a strong household disinfectant before pruning the next bush, as the gall disease can be carried on pruner blades.

Climbing roses should also be pruned at this time. If they have been planted in the last three to five years they will not require drastic pruning—just shorten back each side shoot on the main branches to within two or three buds of the branch. This will promote many good blooms. Then check the support system, making sure that all ties are 25 secure, and that should be all that is required.

Older climbing roses should really have some renewal pruning done. If the rose is multi-stemmed, with perhaps six to eight branches coming from the base, remove one or two of the oldest stems right down at the base of the plant. You will have to untie it and disrupt the rest of the pattern, but the new strong shoots that grow over the summer months will produce wonderful flowers next year and for four or five years to come. In other words, you are replacing growth, at the same time leaving the main part of the climber to give continuous summer blooms.

Once rose pruning is complete and you've collected all the debris, top dress around the root area with a 5-centimetre (2-inch) layer of well-rotted manure or compost. This will not only give the new growth a boost, but will also mulch the roots against the hot summer sun later in the year.

Houseplants from Cuttings

At this time of year houseplants respond to the lengthening days with new growth all over. As soon as this happens you know that any time from now to early May is the right time for taking and rooting houseplant cuttings.

Vegetative propagation is probably the most exciting thing in gardening, next to growing your own seeds. There are many ways to make new plants—from leaves, stems, roots, and regular growth-tip cuttings. Once the knack of taking cuttings is mastered, there's no end to the plants you can swap with friends.

African violets and their close relatives the cape primroses are prime candidates for leaf propagation, along with many types of *Begonia rex*.

26

Many people have great success rooting African violet leaves in water. All you need is a small jar filled with water; a piece of charcoal floating in it helps keep the water sweet. Cover the mouth of the jar with a piece of aluminum foil or clear plastic wrap, securing it with an elastic band, and punch some holes in the covering. Then cut some leaves from your violet, leaving about 5 centimetres (2 inches) of stem on. Place a leaf in each hole so that the base of the stem is well covered by water, and put the jar in a warm, well-lit area where you can watch the roots develop. Once the roots have developed, small plantlets will appear all around the base of the stem. When this happens, remove them from the water, separate each little plant, and plant each one in its own pot. If the water method doesn't work for you, use a rooting medium.

Cape primroses (*Streptocarpus*) are a little different, as they will root from anywhere along the main vein that runs down the centre of the underside of the leaf. This allows one to be a little more adventuresome in the making of the cuttings. These leaves can be anywhere from 20 to 30 centimetres (8 to 12 inches) in length, and by cutting them into seven to ten 3-centimetre (1¼-inch) pieces you can reproduce that many plants. Lay the leaf out flat and cut across it with a sharp knife or razor blade so that each piece has a section of the main vein or midrib running through the middle. Try to keep them in place so that you know which cut is the bottom and which cut is the top. Leaf section cuttings that are placed upside-down in the rooting media will grow eventually, but they root much faster if they are right-side up.

Begonia rex cuttings are taken the same way as violet leaves and are best rooted in a medium. The difference is that instead of producing their new plants from the base of the leaf stem, they send a new plant from the centre of the leaf, right where the stem joins the leaf. With begonias, make the leaf stem fairly short, and bury the cutting right up to the base of the leaf. Otherwise the roots will be at the base of the stem, and the new plant way up at the top.

Stem cuttings of dumb canes, yucca, and some dracaenas work quite well. Dumb cane is the fastest to grow, followed by the dracaenas, while yuccas are very slow and perhaps should be left until mid-April. But the method of making the stem cuttings is the same for all of them.

When the plant is too tall, simply lop it to within 15 centimetres 27

(6 inches) of the soil. Then cut the stem into 7-centimetre (3-inch) sections, removing all leaves. These cuttings are placed on their sides in a seed flat or some similar container, half-buried in a rooting medium. Each section will send out roots from the base and new shoots from every node or leaf joint.

Such plants as aluminum (pilea), freckle plant (hypoestes), and nerve plant (fittonia) are propagated with regular tip cuttings. Take 10-centimetre (4-inch) lengths of the tip growth, and remove the leaves from the lower half, so that at least a couple of leaf joints are exposed for burying in the rooting medium.

The rooting medium for all methods is made up of two parts of open material like perlite or sand to one part of peat, for moisture retention. These two ingredients should be thoroughly mixed and moistened before inserting any cuttings. I don't use rooting hormones with houseplant cuttings, simply because they seem to work quite well without it. But if you have trouble, you could try using a number-one strength, which is specially formulated for softwood cuttings.

The key factors when rooting cuttings are to make sure the mix is kept moist at all times, maintain a good humidity, and provide some bottom heat. Once the cuttings are in their pot or box, they should be covered with clear plastic to keep the moisture in. When I have mixed pots of cuttings, I usually put them inside a plastic bag and seal the top with a tie. Keep them in a warm place, such as the top of the fridge, until they have rooted.

If you have a greenhouse, it is quite likely that you will have an area set aside just for propagation. It can be a shallow wooden box, just large enough to accommodate two seed flats, with a heating cable in the bottom that has a built-in thermostat to keep the rooting mix at around 18°C (66°F). Heating cables are available from garden centres and greenhouse supply shops and can be plugged into regular grounded electrical outlets. Run the cable back and forth across the bottom of the box at 5-centimetre (2-inch) intervals and secure it with nails or staples. Cover the wires with a shallow layer of sand, which provides a more even surface to stand the pots on. Once the cuttings are in place, cover them with a sheet of clear plastic.

28   At this time of year rooting usually takes from ten days to a couple of

weeks. You can tell when rooting has occurred, as the cuttings start to grow. When the root system is the size of a 25-cent piece, you can pot them on.

Gardening for Everyone

With the promise that the growing season isn't too far off, let's give some thought to ways of making gardening easier and possible for everyone. Often people have told me how much they once liked gardening, but they have had to give it up now that they are older and find it difficult to bend. But there are ways of adapting the garden to changing circumstances, so that the joy of gardening can be continued into later years or enjoyed by those who are confined to wheelchairs. Raised gardening beds, an automatic watering system, or a change to container gardening are all ways in which the garden can be adapted.

Now, while the weather is still a little uncertain, is a good time to plan and build some raised beds. A raised garden can be any height you want it to be, so that whether you are in a wheelchair, or like to sit or stand while gardening, the soil level will be comfortable to work with.

Years ago, I was involved in a project to make some raised beds accessible to people in wheelchairs. We used old tables to make beds about 20 centimetres (8 inches) deep and approximately 1 metre wide by 1 ½ metres long (3 feet by 5 feet). The legs of the table allowed wheelchair access. The only problem was that the soil level was too shallow, and once the beds were full of roots they dried out almost hourly during the heat of summer.

We learned from that experience that raised beds that go all the way to ground level work much better, despite the inconvenience of sitting sideways. Sixty-five centimetres (26 inches) is a good average height for

29

working while sitting, and the bed should not be any wider than a metre (3 feet), so that the middle can be reached comfortably from each side. It can be built from lumber, metal, or concrete siding, and don't think that you need to fill it up with good topsoil. As long as the top 30 centimetres (12 inches) is good, the rest can be any soil, just as long as it has decent moisture-retaining quality.

If raised beds are a little too ambitious for you, try some regular planters placed at a comfortable height along a retainer wall or similar structure. Again, remember that they should be no smaller than 30 by 30 centimetres (12 by 12 inches), otherwise they will dry out too quickly.

Larger containers like half-barrels are much better but not easy to move around. However, by adding four casters to the base of each barrel at this time of the year, you will be able to wheel them around your patio to your heart's content this summer.

To make watering easier, there is a marvelous little computerized system manufactured by Gardena, which attaches to a regular faucet and allows you to program up to six different automatic waterings in one day. It retails for just under $100.00.

Container gardening has always been one of my favourite ways to garden because you can locate the pots in specialized locations—hot or shady—creating ideal conditions for exotic and unusual plants. Moreover, there isn't the problem of mowing lawns and trimming hedges, and above all, weeding is cut down to a minimum.

If you haven't tried container gardening and would like some ideas, go to the library and get out some books on the subject. You may end up growing something as exotic as a bougainvillea, or perhaps your best tomatoes ever, in a container this coming year—and never return to traditional gardening.

For more ideas on how to make gardening easier, you can contact an organization in B.C. called DIGA, which stands for Disabled Independent Gardeners Association. Their telephone number is (604) 266-7194.

M A R C H

CHAPTER THREE

Perennials—
Flowers Year after Year

With the mild weather of March, all the early bulbs and blossoms burst forth and the perennials, like the beautiful large oriental poppies, delphiniums, and Michaelmas daisies, start to send up new growth. Even if you don't have any perennials in your garden, this is exactly when you could plan on adding some.

A perennial is a flowering plant that comes up year after year. They are probably the most widely grown group of plants because most of them are completely hardy. Before you get carried away with the thought that this could mean a no-maintenance garden, I must tell you that perennials still need staking, weeding, watering, and fertilizing. They do cut down on the annual cost of bedding plants each spring; however, I believe that the best effect is achieved with a mixture of annuals, bulbs and perennials, so that there is as much colour as possible throughout the growing season.

The new shoots springing up at this time of year tell us that any time now they can be divided and moved, or just cleaned up and fed, depending on their age. If they are older plants that have been in the 31 same place for four years or more, chances are that on a closer look at a Michaelmas daisy, for instance, you will discover that the centre of the clump is almost bare of shoots, rather like a mass of dead stalks with all the new growth ringing the edge. At this stage the plant is ready for dividing.

When you dig out a Michaelmas daisy, you will quickly find out exactly how strong the root system is. If the clumps are more than 30 centimetres (12 inches) across, it may well take two people to dig it up. Once out of the ground, place two long-handled digging forks back to back and force them down through the centre of the clump as close together as possible. Then pull the two handles toward each other, prying the plant apart. If the plant is still too big, then divide the halves again. The pieces can be as small or large as you like; the important thing to remember is to have some roots on each piece.

If you plan to replant a clump in the same spot, add some well-rotted compost or mushroom manure first, working it in to the top 15 centimetres (6 inches) of soil. If you don't want to plant all your clumps, you can swap with a friend for a colour you don't have.

Often when splitting plants, little side shoots will drop off singly. If you have the time, space, and inclination, these can be put into pots or seed flats of rooting mix in a cold frame. After a few weeks, you'll have many more plants—for your local charity plant sale or some other worthy cause.

In younger established perennial beds, where the plants don't need dividing, just weed thoroughly at this time and apply an annual mulch of compost or manure. Be careful not to take too much soil along with the weeds; shake the soil off the roots when you pull them out. I have seen gardeners weeding with a hoe, and then just raking up piles of soil and weeds by the shovelful. Don't—the soil is precious. Once the weeds and all dead stems have been removed, top dress the whole bed with well-rotted manure to a depth of 5 centimetres (2 inches). If you feel the root system needs a boost, spread superphosphate at a handful per square metre (square yard).

You should also know that some perennials, like peonies, are best left undisturbed if they are flowering well, as they tend to sulk for a couple of seasons after being moved. If you do have to move them, always do it in the spring. Lift them carefully, trying to get as much of the long black root as possible, and only repot the roots that have big, fat, white buds at the top, as these are potential flowers. When planting, make sure these buds, or crowns, are just below the surface of the soil; if they are planted too deep, they may never bloom.

If you have a new garden and are just starting from scratch, keep in mind that perennials do well in most soils, but seem to prefer the heavier clay-type soils. To prepare the ground, turn the soil over by hand or with a rototiller to a depth of 30 centimetres (12 inches) or more. Try to get plenty of well-rotted manure into that lower soil and remove perennial weeds, like couch grass and thistle, while digging.

Of course, you will already have planned the size and location of the bed. Perennials like full sun, and since most of them are three to four times the size of the average annual plant, the bed should be at least 2 metres (6 feet) square. Either it will be a long bed against a fence or wall, or an island that can be viewed from all sides. The latter is really nice if you have room, as you can plant taller plants, such as delphiniums, in the middle and shorter plants, such as centaurea and scabious, toward the edges. A nice effect is achieved by leaving fair-sized pockets throughout the bed for a few summer annuals.

There are some good books that deal with planting perennials: *All About Perennials*, by Cort Sinnes, in the Ortho series; *Canadian Garden Perennials*, by A.R. Buckley; and the new *Taylor's Guide to Perennials*, based on the *Taylor's Encyclopedia of Gardening* are just three suggestions. Try to use some perennials in your garden—they are highly rewarding, giving not only a marvelous show of colour outdoors, but providing cut flowers for your home all summer long.

Seed Sowing

Whenever we have a nice sunny March, everyone wants to start sowing seed indoors. While our homes are the ideal temperature for starting seeds, you will run into problems once the seeds are up, unless you have a greenhouse. For those who do have a greenhouse or cold frame, now is the time to start thinking about seed for your garden this year, particularly for some of the annuals that need a longer period to develop, such as petunias, snapdragons, and impatiens.

First you will need pots or containers to sow in. Ten-centimetre (4-inch) pots or individual-sized yogurt containers with holes punched in the bottom for drainage work very well. Don't get carried away with sowing seeds; remember that a thinly sown pot this size can produce up to 150 seedlings.

Next you'll need some good soil. Either purchase a sterilized potting mix from a garden centre or make your own of equal parts soil, peat, and sand. For soil, you can use screened topsoil from your garden or well-rotted compost. The sand should be coarse, almost gravelly (river sand works well). Screen the peat to get rid of some of the sticks and fibre, and pre-moisten the peat (use hot water; it's absorbed faster by dry peat than cold water).

Mix all the ingredients well, then sterilize your homemade mix. You can do this by steaming it or by baking it in a 200°C (425°F) preheated oven in a sealed container with foil wrapped tightly around to keep in the smell and moisture. Use an old meat thermometer to check the inside temperature of the soil. When it reaches 90°C (195°F) it should be removed at once and spread to cool on a clean surface. This treatment will ensure that fungus spores are killed and weeds don't germinate along with your seeds. Don't think that you'll be able to pull out the weeds. Believe me, when seedlings are tiny, they all look the same—even to a trained eye.

Whether you're using homemade or ready mixed soil, you'll have to add a little fertilizer to it. For seed mixes, the traditional one is super-phosphate, which is used by plants to build up a healthy root system.

Fifteen millilitres (1 tablespoon) per level household pailful of soil should be enough, as all the rest of the elements necessary for germination are stored within the seed itself.

When filling your pots, the mix should be nice and moist, but not muddy. If the drainage holes seem too large, place some paper towelling over them before filling. Tip the soil mix in lightly, mounding it slightly, then smooth it off level with the rim of the pot. Use the bottom of another container to push it down, making a level sowing surface; this is most important for good, even germination.

Now you're ready to sow. Seed size varies from species to species and you'll find with lobelia or begonia, for instance, that the seed is extremely fine, so watch that you don't sneeze while it is in the palm of your hand. I like to mix very fine seed with some fine dry sand before sowing—it seems to help spread it more uniformly. Tomato seed is larger, and I know some people who actually sow it individually with tweezers, so that it is really evenly spaced. I just shake the seed into the palm of my hand, then tilt it slightly and tap it with my other hand, and the seed falls evenly and gently onto the level surface.

When covering the seeds with soil, do it so lightly that you can still see the seed showing through. If the seeds are covered too deeply they push up great tents of mix when they germinate, and this often causes rot before they get a chance to push through the surface. To apply this layer evenly and gently, you can make a sieve with a small box that has a fine mesh stapled onto the bottom (or you can use a recycled flour sifter). When germination takes place it is easy to add a little more soil to cover the developing roots.

Some seed germinates best if covered with a piece of dark plastic and other seed needs light; you'll have to experiment a bit. In the past, I've covered each pot with a sheet of glass, which was turned each day to check for moisture and germination.

Once the seedlings are up, get them into as much light as possible, but if you're setting them on a window sill, watch for the heat of the sun around midday. It is already hot enough in March to burn the tender seedlings very quickly. When the sun is hot, protect the plants with a double layer of cheesecloth or a sheet of newspaper. Artificial light can also work well. A combination of cool white and warm white fluores- 35 cent tubes placed 30 centimetres (12 inches) above the seedlings is ideal.

The temperature should be on the cooler side—12°C (54°F) at night and 15° to 17° (60° to 64°F) during the day. If it is any warmer the seedlings will bolt and become weak, so that they eventually rot. When the seedlings are large enough to pick up carefully by hand—in two or three weeks—they are ready for transplanting, which is discussed in the April section, on page 42.

Meanwhile, have fun with your sowing; tomatoes, lettuce, leeks, onions, asters, zinnias, cosmos, and petunias are some seeds you could be sowing, to name a few. And remember, if your seedlings don't work out, the garden centres always have plenty of back-up plants when May planting time arrives.

Peas and Broad Beans

When cherries, plums, and forsythia are in full bloom, and the weeds begin to thrive, it means the soil is warm enough to put in some peas and broad beans.

If you haven't already prepared your soil, remember that peas and beans are fairly deep-rooted, so your manure or compost should be turned under to at least 30 and up to 45 centimetres (12 to 18 inches). Put the fertilizer just along the row, and to a width of about 60 centimetres (2 feet), which is the width that the roots will spread.

While you're digging in the soil, make sure you take out any perennial weeds, such as dandelion, nettle, and bitter cress (and don't put them in the compost!). After the area is prepared, walk lightly over it to settle the soil. If you don't do this now, the rains will do it later, causing an uneven surface and erratic growth.

The secret to germinating peas is to soak them for three to four hours in a glassful of water on your kitchen counter. The next day, you'll see that they've doubled in size. Drain off the water and place the seeds between several sheets of wet paper towelling or newspaper on an old pie dish. Keep them on your kitchen counter or somewhere handy so that you can watch them carefully and keep the paper wet. Within two days, the seeds will be showing their new little root tips and at this stage it is crucial to keep them moist. Within another day or two they'll be ready for planting into individual peat pots or right into the garden, under a protective plastic cloche.

Plastic cloches can be very useful for early sowing. If you put them up a month before the recommended sowing date in your area and keep the plastic tightly closed, it results in early warming of the soil. With this method, you can sow up to two or three weeks ahead of time.

Once the seeds are up, make sure to raise the plastic on one side on sunny days to allow for ventilation, but remember to close it again about an hour before sunset to trap the heat. Vegetables grown by this method will be ready for harvesting three weeks before the normal picking date.

When the peas and beans are ready to be planted out in their rows, plant them 10 centimetres (4 inches) apart in double rows about 45 centimetres (18 inches) apart. If you plan ahead, you'll know the length of your rows and how many seeds you'll need to sprout so you don't end up wasting a lot (this is one of my major faults; I always prepare too many seeds).

There are a couple of varieties of broad beans that are worth growing. 'Broad Windsor' has been around for years and a more recent introduction is 'Brunette', which has smaller, brown-seeded, upright-growing pods. Perhaps you have to be of English origin to love broad beans, but you haven't lived until you've had them early in the season, lightly steamed and served with parsley sauce!

There are many wonderful peas to choose from, including the tender 'Sugar Snap'. You can eat pod and all of this variety; even when the pod is full of peas they don't get stringy. If you like traditional 'Snow Peas' for stir-fry, then try 'Norli' for a good early crop. For regular early peas, there is 'Early May' which comes on 60-centimetre (2-foot) vines as early as June. The nice thing about this variety is that any older peas can be dried and used as yellow dried peas for winter soups and stews.

For those living in apartments with balconies or patios, it is possible to grow very tasty peas in pots, and 'Little Marvel' is a good variety. Be careful, though, if you're using those large black plastic nursery pots, to shield the pots from the sun as the days warm up. Peas hate warm soil.

Herbs for Your Garden

With the arrival of spring, there is much to plan for the season ahead. But when you're planning, try not to forget herbs. Even if you don't cook with them they are very pleasant to have around, both for colour and scent.

Many herbs can be grown from seed, such as parsley, chives, and basil, but it might be simpler to purchase the more difficult varieties from a local grower. In the lower mainland of B.C., Tansy Farms have just about every herb you can think of and they will ship throughout the province. Write to Box 1126, Stn. A, Surrey, B.C., V3S 4P6; or phone (604) 576-2785.

When choosing a site for your herb garden, remember that the majority of herbs love well-drained soil and lots of sun—not surprising, as many of them come from lovely warm climates, such as Greece. The fact that the soil should be well drained does not rule out the necessity for nutrition. As with all spring planting, the addition of manure or compost is beneficial.

It's also a good idea to situate your herb garden close to the house, so that you don't have to go to the bottom of the garden in the rain, when you need a herb for something you're cooking.

The herbs that you grow will depend on your taste, of course. But if you're not sure, then let me suggest a few. Sage comes in many forms and different leaf colours—grey, purple and variegated, the grey giving the best flavour. (For those who have always wondered, the sagebrush of the interior is not used for culinary purposes. Perhaps the pioneers named it sage because it reminded them of the edible plant back home.) With sage, not only are the leaves good, but the flowers are a beautiful bluish purple. It is so showy in the early summer that it could well be used in a flower border.

Chives also have the bonus of lovely flowers. They are typical of the onion family, global in shape, and a lovely shade of purple. The flowers themselves can really brighten up a salad, and are also delicious and attractive in an omelette. Many people have the misconception that when chives have bloomed the foliage is no longer good to eat. Not so—in fact, after chives have flowered, cut half the clump right back to the ground. Soon tasty new leaves will grow up from the cut part. When they are ready to use, cut the other half back, giving a continuous supply of new growth.

Basil is another favourite, but it really needs the heat. In fact, it isn't safe to set basil out until the end of June, and even then, it won't be happy if the nights are cool. But for the best homemade pesto you must grow basil.

While mint is a lovely herb, be warned, it is extremely invasive and should not be planted with other herbs unless the roots are checked in some way. One method is to sink a bottomless bucket or other cylinder into the ground with the rim about 5 centimetres (2 inches) above the soil surface. Plant your mint inside it, and the rest of your garden will be safe.

All herbs lend themselves to sunny balcony or patio planting, and grow well in half-barrels and pots. An attractive way to grow herbs is to use a strawberry pot—the pots from Mexico or Italy with a series of pockets for planting in the sides. They come in different sizes. A good size for growing herbs will stand about 60 centimetres (2 feet) high with perhaps nine pockets in the side and room for three plants in the top.

The secret to successful herb-growing in pots is watering. When using strawberry pots, you have to specially prepare the pot with a conductor tube down the centre. First, put some drainage material in the bottom. It can be old styrofoam cups or cut-up plastic flower pots. Then fill to the first layer of holes with good outdoor potting soil and select and plant your herbs. Place them down inside the pot and poke them out through the holes. Now get a piece of pipe and cut it so that it will reach the soil level at the top of the pot when its base is sitting on the first layer of soil that you have just added. Drill some holes in the side of the pipe to make it more effective.

Continue to fill around the pipe, planting each time you reach the next level of holes. When you reach the top, firm the soil well, leaving enough space between the soil level and the rim for watering, and plant your last three herbs. Almost all herbs are suitable for planting in a pot (except mint, of course, which needs a pot all to itself).

Planting Roses

When the first day of spring and the long Easter weekend are nearby, it is a good time to visit your local garden centre to check out their nursery stock, particularly shrubs and roses. In milder areas, we usually plant roses in October or November, but container-grown roses come into the garden centres now.

When planting roses, remember that they like fairly heavy but well-drained soil, so if your garden soil is sandy and well-drained, incorporate as much organic matter in the preparation of a rose bed as you can. You can use well-rotted manure or compost or even moist peat. As a general rule, roses do well in a bed devoted just to them, but they can also do well planted here and there as a highlight in a mixed flower border.

Dig the hole for your new rose before you remove it from the container, making it twice the diameter of the container and one and a half times deeper. This allows room to add some good soil and compost under the rose, which encourages good strong new root growth.

Roses and other shrubs are usually sold in papier-mâché-type pots, which the manufacturer claims will rot if planted. They do rot, but they take a long time—over a year, in fact. This is not desirable, as it can cause waterlogging or severe drying depending on the season, so you should carefully remove the pots. Always water the plant well the night before, or at least three hours before, so that the soil adheres to the root ball when the container is removed. The key with roses is to not disturb the root ball.

Carefully remove it from the pot and place it in the prepared hole, so that the bump on the lower part of the bush (which indicates where the graft was made) is just above the soil surface. Finally, fill in around the root ball with good soil that has manure or compost worked into it. As you fill in, gently firm it with your foot as you go. When you've finished, water it in well.

If your pot-grown rose has been planted in a sawdust mix, most of the mix will just fall away when you remove the pot, revealing a rather sparse root system with some new white growth starting to appear here and there. If this happens, get the bush planted right away and when placing it in the hole, try to spread the roots gently and carefully out across the soil. Firm the soil around the roots with your fingers, finishing up with your foot at the very end. This method also works with bare root rose bushes.

Shrubs are dealt with in exactly the same way. The key factor to note is that the plant is never buried deeper than it was originally in the container. However, it shouldn't end up higher out of the ground either, as anything planted on a hill is extremely difficult to water.

Water, of course, is especially important to any newly planted growth. After the first watering in, mulch the root area with compost or other well-rotted organic material to cut down on water evaporation; then make sure that you continue to water on a regular basis throughout the first growing season.

A P R I L

CHAPTER FOUR

Transplanting Seedlings

If you sowed your seeds for the summer garden last month, it's now time to transplant those seedlings that have been growing steadily on your windowsill or under lights.

Seed sowing mix has very little fertilizer in it, aside from a little phosphate perhaps. But transplanting mix needs those added nutrients to give the seedlings a big boost and get them ready for the garden. Any good sterile potting mix will do, but check to see if it already has some added fertilizer—some garden centres mix their own and add fertilizer. If it already has fertilizer in it, don't add more. Too much fertilizer can burn the roots at this stage. For the plain mix, add about 30 millilitres (2 tablespoons) of granular 6-8-6 or 4-10-10 to a household pailful of mix.

If you're making your own transplanting mix, the proportions are three parts soil, two parts peat and one part sand. All should be thoroughly mixed and moistened and then sterilized, as outlined on page 34. Once your soil is ready and your pots assembled, you're ready to go. This mix is also good for repotting houseplants.

42   If you were tempted to sow your seeds too early, or your growing

light was poor, chances are your plants could be very leggy, or drawn and thin. If this is the case, the individual seedlings will just fall over when they're separated out and planted. To solve this, there is a little trick you can do with seedlings that you can't do with older established plants. Seedlings can be buried deeper—right up to the first set of leaves, in fact. The soil will support them, and because they are seedlings, they'll root from the stem.

Depending on your plants, you'll either transplant into individual 10-centimetre (4-inch) pots or you'll reuse those plastic baskets that you saved from last year's purchased bedding plants. (Ten plants will fit into one of these baskets.) Before adding any soil, cover the drainage holes with a layer of paper towelling.

In the old days we called our homemade tools for transplanting dibbers and widgers. A widger was usually an old teaspoon or popsicle stick, used for lifting the seedlings gently out of their seed pot. The dibber was used for making the holes for the roots in the new potting mix. I find that an old ballpoint pen or pencil works fine for this.

Lift the seedlings carefully, then separate them gently, so that you can pick each one up and drop it into the prepared hole. Cover it to its seed leaves, or lowest leaves, and lightly firm the soil around it with your dibber. Don't forget to label your pots as you do them.

You'll find that some plants, like tomatoes, for instance, are easy to separate because they have good strong stems and two classic seed leaves at the top. But smaller seedlings, like lobelia or fibrous rooted begonias, are virtually impossible to single out, and are usually transplanted as tiny clumps. This explains why there sometimes appear to be different coloured flowers from the same plant; in reality there are several plants together.

Place the newly potted plants in good light but away from direct sun, especially for the first few days, when they will tend to wilt from root loss during transplanting. There comes a time when conditions in the house are just too hot, and it is at this stage that you need a cool greenhouse or a cold frame.

A cold frame is quick and easy to make and can be as simple as a temporary frame made with wooden sides and a heavy-gauge plastic top. Place it in a sheltered spot in good light and open the top on sunny days, closing it an hour before the sun goes down to trap heat for the night. If it is unseasonably cold, add an extra cover at night.

Plants grown this way will be much more hardy and acclimatized when it comes to planting time in May. A lot of seedlings come straight from a warm greenhouse to our gardens, where the temperatures may drop more than 10 degrees overnight—causing the poor plants to turn reddish or blue with the cold. For more information on building and using cold frames, see page 55.

Planning a Fruit Garden

Fresh fruit from the garden is always a delight, and even the smallest garden can afford a small space allotted to the pleasure of picking a few sun-warmed berries and popping them into your mouth, or munching on the freshest possible apple.

No matter where you live in B.C., this is a good month to plant fruit trees. There are various sources for purchasing fruit trees, including a specialist nursery on Saltspring Island called Hallman Orchards and Nursery. It is interesting because it carries many of the old apple varieties that used to be grown more widely and are now rarely seen.

All fruit-bearing plants require as much sunshine as possible and should be planted well away from other trees and buildings. If they are trained fruit trees, grow them against a south- or southeast-facing wall for maximum exposure to sunlight.

The soil should be well drained, not a low area that becomes flooded during the winter months. If the only space you have is poorly drained, raise the bed 30 centimetres (12 inches) or so. When preparing the soil 44 for fruit, dig in plenty of well-rotted manure or compost and mix it through to a depth of 60 centimetres (2 feet).

Strawberries do well on south-facing slopes and should be planted 45 centimetres (18 inches) apart. When selecting plants, make sure they have some new foliage growth on them, and when planting, take care not to cover the crown or growth tip. If planted too deep, the crowns can rot. In addition to the manure that has already been dug in, fertilize the area at planting time with granular 6-8-6 or bone-meal, sprinkling a handful per square metre (square yard).

In theory, the blossoms that occur this first season should be removed to discourage fruiting, which weakens the plant. However, this is extremely hard to do, so if you do let them fruit, feed the plants once a month in July and August to build them up for the following season.

Raspberries are not as deeply rooted as some of the other fruits, and should have some compost or manure worked into the surface area. The planting trench should only be 7 centimetres (3 inches) deep. As well as the traditional row method, raspberries can be planted tepee-style around a central pole, or in two rows about 1½ metres (5 feet) apart, which are then trained in an A-frame style (forming a tent which children love to crawl inside to harvest the berries).

In traditional row planting the rows should run north-south, providing equal light to both sides of the row. Plant the canes 45 centimetres (18 inches) apart and approximately 7 centimetres (3 inches) deep, spreading the roots out horizontally. Cover the roots with soil and firm them in with your foot. Once planted, the canes should be pruned back to 15 centimetres (6 inches) above soil level. This will encourage strong shoots from the base, forming the fruiting canes for the following year. To support the canes, use a post and wire system which is probably easier to erect before planting but which can also be done in the fall.

When it comes time to select the fruit trees for your garden, you'll find that there are many dwarf varieties of apples and pears that are most suitable to today's smaller home garden. With the dwarf varieties, the fruit is grafted onto a dwarf rootstock, which is a much less vigorous root system. It produces a smaller tree that still bears adequate amounts of fruit and the fruit is easy to reach for harvesting. At the UBC Botanical Garden there are a whole range of fruit trees on display in the food garden. My favourite is a 'Golden Delicious' apple tree that is grafted onto a 'Malling 27' rootstock. The tree is no more than a metre (3 feet) in height and last year it had over twenty full-sized tasty apples on it. It is so tiny that every time I saw it, I wanted to pat it and say, "Well done!"

Most apple, pear, peach, cherry, and plum trees sold at this time of the year come bare root, or with their roots wrapped in moist sawdust and burlap. If you purchase trees this way, it is important not to let the roots dry out, so as soon as you get them home, heel them in. This means burying their roots in soil temporarily, until you are ready to plant them.

Having selected your tree and heeled it in if necessary, it will be time to prepare the hole for planting. Dig the hole twice as deep as the root area, and if possible, twice as wide. In the bottom, mix some well-rotted manure or compost into the soil.

Next, hold the new tree in place, making sure that the bump on the lower part of the trunk is slightly higher than the soil level around it. Why is this so important? The bump is the graft, and if it is buried, roots will be encouraged to grow from above it, causing the tree to lose its dwarf characteristics. When you have the soil at the right level, hold on to your tree with one hand while you fill in the soil around it. Shake it up and down now and then, to settle the soil around and between the roots. Once the hole is filled, firm the soil in gently but firmly with your foot and stake it for the first couple of seasons.

The traditional European styles of fruit growing, espalier or cordon, are also ideal for the small garden. An espalier is several carefully pruned layered branches supported by a wire frame or a fence. A cordon is a single-stemmed tree, pruned to bear fruit all the way up the stem. If you are planning to train your tree into one of these shapes, prune the top back severely to encourage good strong growth from the dormant growth buds on the lower part of the trunk. Espaliers and cordons require specialized pruning and training, but it is challenging and fun to do. I strongly recommend the *RHS Guide to Practical Gardening*, published by Simon and Schuster. The volume on fruit has step-by-step diagrams, and easy to follow text that makes fruit tree training possible for everyone.

Spring Pruning of Flowering Trees and Shrubs

Whenever most gardeners think of pruning, they think of fall and winter, when everything is dormant. But with many ornamental flowering trees and shrubs, the best time for pruning is right after they've flowered.

Forsythia is one of the most widely known and grown spring flowering shrubs in British Columbia. Whenever I see forsythia trimmed into the shape of a round ball or a hedge, I always feel so sad, because if it's left in its natural shape it will give the most spectacular fountain of gold display every March or April.

This is because the best flowers occur on the previous season's new wood—the shoots that appear like long fishing poles during May and June. If you are new to gardening, there is often an urge to cut them off, which leaves only old wood and fewer flowering buds for next spring. Instead, as soon as the flowers have faded, get out your good sharp pruners and prune out some or most of the older branches. Prune them way back, as close to the ground as possible.

Something to keep in mind when you are cutting branches of forsythia, or any other flowering bush, for flower arrangements, is to cut carefully, pruning the bush as you cut your blossoms. So often we are in a rush and just cut random pieces here and there. If you cut a piece, leaving the cut end way out near the edge of the bush, you will get masses of those long shoots appearing in the early summer, just below where the cut has been made, making a very lopsided bush.

Another close runner-up for popularity is chaenomeles, or Japanese flowering quince. Many people just refer to it as japonica, but that name is only used as a species name and means that the plant originally came from Japan (hence *Camellia japonica*, *Fatsia japonica*, etc.). Flowering quince have gorgeous red flowers in clusters, resembling the form of apple blossoms. They also occur on the previous year's growth, and the shrub can be pruned like forsythia. Flowering quince lends itself well to being trained against a wall or fence, and if it is, new shoots   47 appear on and off throughout the growing season. They will need their first trimming back when they start to grow after the flowering, but just cut them back to within two leaf buds of their point of origin. This means that there are little spurs of new growth left. By June they will need trimming again, and once more in August. Those spurs that are left will be dense with flowers next spring.

A climbing vine that will be blooming soon in the late spring is wisteria. Many people have trouble getting it to bloom, but proper pruning can solve that problem. After blooming time, wisteria sends out masses of new shoots, which are long climbing shoots. If your vine has reached the size you want it to be, these shoots can be cut back to within two or three leaf buds, much like the espalier method of pruning Japanese flowering quince. This pruning will help produce flowering spurs for the following season.

Another spring bloomer is magnolia. As a general rule, they do not require much pruning unless they've been planted in the wrong place and a branch or two is intruding into a walkway or driveway. If that is the case, then now is the time to prune. When pruning, don't just cut the tips; go right back to the source of the branch. In the case of the more tree-like magnolias, like *M. soulangiana* or *M. kobus* a pruning saw will be required. For big cuts, use pruning paint immediately after the cut is made, both for aesthetic reasons and to prevent disease from entering the cut.

While on the subject of magnolias, if you are putting in a new garden this year and would like a magnolia that doesn't grow too fast or take up too much room, select a *Magnolia stellata*, or star magnolia. It is a beauty.

Camellias should also be pruned at this time, although they may only need light pruning. Just because they are thought to be somewhat exotic, don't be frightened to cut them. They tend to form rather a tight growth habit, so don't just cut off the shoots that look out of place or that are hanging over the sidewalk. To promote new shoots from the centre of the bush rather than the outside, follow that shoot to the base and cut it right back to the centre of the bush.

People often ask when to prune rhododendrons. The answer is that you don't. But once again, that cute small rhododendron in the nursery pot might have grown to be a giant over the years. Rhododendrons love the coastal climate and grow quite rapidly. So if it is a beautiful specimen that has outgrown its surroundings, I would recommend moving it if at all possible, either now or in the fall.

If this isn't possible then you will have to prune, but you should be aware that rhododendrons take two or three years to produce new flowering wood. Prune right after flowering, and cut the branches that are in the way right back to the centre of the bush. Try to prune just every other branch, so that the whole shrub is not denuded and the newly cut branches have some time to form new shoots. Next year do the other half. But please be warned that this is a drastic pruning and not recommended.

Once any large-flowered shrubs have finished blooming, it is a good idea to pick off the deadheads, rather than let them form seed. Removing rhododendron deadheads is a sticky business, and you must be careful to break them in the right place. Don't take off the growth buds that are right below the bloom, as they will be next year's flowers.

Finally, just a reminder that any trees or shrubs that have flowered in the spring and are just developing new growth at this time will most definitely appreciate a feeding right now. I favour seaweed or fish-based fertilizers, which may be mixed at half the recommended rate and given every couple of weeks through to the middle of June. If some of your shrubs haven't bloomed too well, despite the fact that they were in good light, then give them a fertilizer that has a higher middle and last number. The last number, which is potash, will promote flowering.

Planning a Cut Flower Border

All the old stately homes of Europe had large perennial flower gardens, particularly in England, where they were always referred to as herbaceous borders. Perennials are the flowering plants that come 49 up year after year, such as delphiniums, phlox, asters, oriental poppies, and many more. They are becoming much more widely available here now, and can form the basis for a cut flower border or garden.

All perennials like a rich soil, and if yours is poorly drained, you will need to add plenty of organic matter to the soil, not only to nourish the plants, but also to retain moisture. For most home gardens, it is most likely that you will have one flower border where everything from spring bulbs to annuals are grown and perennials bloom in the in-between periods of June, August and September. When planning your perennial planting, acquaint yourself with the height the mature plants will reach. Then you can make sure the tall ones are kept to the back of the bed or border, or the middle of a circular bed.

Most purchased perennials come either bare root in a plastic bag or in 10-centimetre (4-inch) pots. When preparing the soil, dig a hole at least twice the size of the root area and if possible twice as deep. If you have a hard-pan problem, then over-compensate a little by widening the width. First, work well-rotted manure or compost through the soil to be added around the plant. If the roots are bare, fill in the hole a bit, and spread the roots as much as possible, holding the crowns or growing tips just a bit below the level of the surrounding soil area. As you fill in the soil, lightly shake the roots up and down to settle the soil around and between them. Finally, lightly firm the soil around the plant with your foot. If the soil is very wet, do it with your fingers to avoid harmful soil compaction. When you're finished the plant should be in a slight depression for ease of watering.

For many years, perennials were out of favour simply because they needed staking, but there are easy ways of dealing with that. Cut some saplings of birch or alder into lengths just a little less than the potential height of your plants. Stick them in the ground all around the plant, and even between the branches, and the plant will grow up through the twigs, eventually hiding the supports.

Delphiniums are high on my list of perennial favourites because they are blue. They do need staking however, and be sure to be generous with the manure or compost.

Lupins are another choice. The native blue ones grow throughout B.C., but do try some of the old 'Russell Hybrids' if you can get them.

They are very pretty and are excellent for cutting.

Later on in the summer, any of the heleniums are good. They also need staking but if you like yellows and orange tones, then you must grow some. For fall cutting, no garden would be complete without the perennial asters or Michaelmas daisies. They are predominantly blue or magenta and range in height from 30 centimetres to a metre (1 to 3 feet).

Planting annuals each year can add the spice of variety to a good perennial border, and you'll always have beautiful cut flowers for your home. Some bedding plants to watch for are the annual asters. They come in various forms, and range in colour from white through blues, purples, and pinks. I particularly love the single daisy type for cutting. They reach a mature height of around 40 centimetres (16 inches), so they shouldn't be planted too far in from the edge in a mixed bed.

Sweet peas are among the best producers of summer flowers, and while traditionally they have always been grown in rows, they may also be planted in clumps, in a mixed flower border, or on a circle of chicken wire. If your garden isn't suited to climbing peas, there are many short-growing forms to choose from which do not require staking, but still produce stems long enough for cutting.

If you have had trouble growing sweet peas in the past, try adding some Nature's Aid granular garden inoculant. It contains nitrogen-fixing microbes, which safely supply nitrogen fertilization to all members of the pea and bean family. It is primarily used on crop plants, but will also do wonders for flowering peas. If it is almost too late to start sweet peas from seed, there are plenty of bedding plants in the garden centres at this time of year.

If you'd like to try growing something from seed, there is still time to grow zinnias. Seeds sown now will be ready for planting out in late May. Zinnias are heat-loving annuals that need a good sunny spot in the garden and tend to bloom later in the summer. They reach about 45 centimetres (18 inches) when fully mature, producing wonderful cuttings during August and early September.

There are some annuals that can be sown directly into the soil as it warms up. One of my all-time favourites is larkspur, which is really an annual delphinium. It has fine feathery leaves and 60-centimetre-high 51

(2-foot-high) flower spikes that range through all the pastel shades. Clarkia is a close second, vying with bachelor's buttons.

Hanging Baskets

British Columbia hanging baskets are quite famous the world over, particularly the ones in Victoria, the Butchart Gardens and Kelowna. It's still too early to put out your bedding plants but now is the time to get a head start on the season with your hanging baskets, so that when it comes time to put them outside, around the third week of May, they will have that nice established look. However, in order for early planting to be successful, you'll need a cold frame, cool greenhouse, or a room in your house with lots of light, where the temperature can be controlled. It should be no warmer than 18°C (65°F) by day and somewhere around 10°C (50°F) at night.

One of the major problems with hanging baskets is the fact that they dry out so quickly in the summer months. There are several steps you can take to help the retention of moisture in your basket, and first and foremost is the size of the basket. Those small plastic baskets that have been on the market for years, measuring less than 30 centimetres (12 inches) across the top, are really difficult to care for, simply because they do not have room for the volume of soil needed to retain moisture.

Much better are open-sided cedar baskets, 45 by 30 centimetres (18 by 12 inches) and 25 centimetres (10 inches) deep, and wire baskets that measure 45 centimetres (18 inches) across and are 30 centimetres (12 inches) at the top narrowing to 15 centimetres (6 inches). Both these types are lined with moss before filling, and if the moss is packed firmly enough, it will also help hold the moisture.

There is also a product available called Terra Sorb. It looks like large sugar crystals. When water is added, these crystals store up to 400 times their weight in water, forming gel-like water chunks. The manufacturers claim that when added to potting mixes, these lumps can slowly release water to your plants over days or weeks. I have tried it and it works very well.

When it comes to lining your baskets with moss, it is perfectly all right to use moss raked from your lawn; just make sure you take all the grass out, otherwise it will grow well in your basket all summer long. It takes quite a bit of moss to line a basket properly. Make up small balls of moss and squeeze them tightly between the wire or wood. If you just lay it inside in loose sheets it will fall apart when you add the potting mix.

Before putting any mix in the baskets, either put a piece of plastic in the bottom to form a tray about 3 centimetres (1½ inches) deep, or use a plastic saucer inside the base of the basket (an idea borrowed from the successful hanging-basket-makers of Victoria).

The soil mix should be fairly peaty in its composition to help retain moisture. A good test is to fill a pot with moist mix and water it. If the water goes straight through and out the bottom quickly, you definitely need more peat in the mix. If you're making your own mix, use one part soil, two parts peat and about half a part of sand or perlite. Moisten the mix well before filling the basket and don't bother adding granular fertilizer to the mix; instead use regular liquid feedings of either 20-20-20 or seaweed fertilizer throughout the summer.

For a basket that looks good instantly, use plants that have been grown in individual 7- or 10-centimetre (3- or 4-inch) pots. Plant them in thickly (so that all the root balls are touching), about twenty-four plants for a 45- by 30-centimetre (18- by 12-inch) basket.

On the edges of the basket plant trailers, such as lobelia or verbena. If you have periwinkle in your garden, lift a bit for the basket. Trailing fuchsias are also wonderful for baskets as their delicate blossoms can be seen from below, not to mention their ability to attract humming-birds, which can keep you entertained all summer. Experiment a bit in the centre. Along with old standards for hanging baskets, like pelargoniums and petunias, try adding parsley, chives, sage or other herbs. Or make an entire basket of ornamental herbs, one of strawber-ries, another of 'Tiny Tim' tomatoes. The possibilities are endless.

Once planted, fill in the gaps with more potting mix, leaving enough   53 room between the surface of the soil and the rim of the pot for watering. Once the plants have established a decent root system, start feeding weak solutions of your favourite liquid fertilizer twice a week, stepping up to every other day in the height of summer. When it comes time to put the baskets outside, hang them away from full sun, perhaps under the eaves.

It is a lot of work to plant and maintain hanging baskets. But the pleasure you will get, not just from planting but also from creating your own miniature hanging gardens, can be highly rewarding.

Bedding Plants

It never ceases to amaze me how quickly all the large grocery stores produce their bedding plants out front, just as soon as the sun shines. It is always too early. I recall seeing some sad-looking petunias that had probably come from a greenhouse with a temperature of 22°C (72°F) and had gone through a night of 3° (38°F) temperatures. They were blue-green with the cold.

If you have put your bedding plants out too early you will have observed that they turned a deep purple or reddish colour overnight. To find out why, just take your favourite chair out on the lawn about 11 p.m., don't put on any extra coats or sweaters, and see how long it takes before you turn blue!

Seriously, it is always tempting at this time of year to get the plants into the garden, but be very careful about which plants you choose, and how and when you do it. It is very important to harden bedding plants off. They can take a few weeks to recover from the shock of going straight from a warm greenhouse to a cold night outside. I can hear you saying that you have to purchase your plants early or the best selection will be gone. It's probably true that public demand does start the rush, so if you must purchase your bedding plants early, keep them in a cold frame for at least a couple more weeks.

Cold frames facilitate the transition from the warmth of a greenhouse or indoor situation to the reality of the cold outdoors, and they are quite easy to build. A typical size for a home cold frame is 1 metre by 2 metres (3 feet by 6 feet), with a depth of 45 centimetres (18 inches) on the back to 30 centimetres (12 inches) at the front. (The angle is so that the glass or plastic can be slanted toward the rays of the sun.) Old windows can be used for the top if you have any around. If not, clear heavy-gauge polyethylene secured to a wooden frame is just as good. You may have to have an anchoring mechanism for the latter if your area is windy, as the light plastic top can be lifted by a strong wind. Some people hinge the top at the back so it can be propped open, but I prefer a top that can be taken right off or one that slides up and down, for better air circulation.

It's a good idea to make your cold frame portable, so it can be moved to sheltered or sunnier areas depending on your requirement. At this time of year, it's better to have it away from full sun as the sun is getting stronger and can burn the seedlings.

Place as many plants as you can in the cold frame, making sure that there's enough space between each flat or basket to allow good air circulation. If it's not sunny at first, keep the top closed all the time, but as soon as the sun appears, open the top a bit to allow the excess heat out. Remember to close it one hour before sunset to retain heat for the night. The longer the plants are in the cold frame, the more air should be given. After about two weeks of coddling you can start leaving the top open a crack at night, so that the plants have a gradual introduction to the cold. That process is what gardeners call hardening off.

If you live in an apartment and don't have room for a cold frame, there are all sorts of ingenious inventions that serve the same purpose. I've seen recycled clear plastic umbrellas used as a dome and deep sturdy cardboard cartons with a plastic cover for the top.

Although it's still too early to bed out the plants, the warm weather at the end of April is ideal for working the soil into what old English gardeners call "a fine tilth," in preparation for planting out and sowing the first seeds of hardy varieties. This means repeated raking to level the soil and break all the large lumps down into fine pieces. For soil that   55 has been recently dug, walk backwards and forwards over the area to settle it. Just before planting, scatter some general granular fertilizer, like 6-8-6, at a handful per square metre (square yard) before raking. If the neighborhood cats find your freshly raked soil attractive, make sure you cover the area once its sown with chickenwire netting or some twiggy sticks, at least until the seedlings are up and large enough to survive cat paws.

Having made my point about not putting plants out too early, I should tell you that there are some hardy plants that can go into the garden now, if you live in an area with a mild climate. First-time gardeners often find it difficult to understand why some vegetables and flowers, such as peas, sweet peas, and broccoli, can go out earlier than others. Probably the best way to understand it is to think of the native environments of plants. Some plants come from cooler areas of the world and can tolerate more cold, whereas corn, cucumbers, and tomatoes are more tropical in origin. Toward the end of May is quite early enough for most plants unless you are growing them under plastic cloches.

The hardier species that can go into the ground now if it is warm enough in your area are peas, carrots, onions and cabbages, the latter being available as bedding plants from your local garden centre. In fact, you may already have your peas and beans in the ground, or protected under plastic. For directions on germinating and planting them, see page 37.

Potatoes can also be started now. Plant them in shallow trenches 15 centimetres (6 inches) deep, and contrary to popular belief, well-rotted manure can be added to the soil. The main problem to watch for with potatoes is scab, which is a soil-borne fungus often activated by putting too much lime in the soil. Don't add any lime to your potato area, and if scab has been a problem in the past, try 'Netted Gem' or 'Norgold', both of which are scab-resistant.

M A Y

CHAPTER FIVE

Planting-out and Sowing Time

May is here at last and all those chomping at the bit to get planting can finally get out into the garden to sow and plant the more hardy flowers and vegetables. Towards the end of the month or early in June, depending on the weather and your location, even the most tender varieties can be planted out in most areas.

If you haven't tried them before, why not plant some of those little early sweet beets. A couple of good early varieties are 'Little Mini Ball' and 'Little Egypt'. The greens are delicious and the beets are eaten while they are about the size of a fifty-cent piece in diameter and still sweet.

First make a seed drill a little less than a centimetre (¼ inch) deep, using a line or a straight-edged board to get the row straight. Sow the seed thinly, approximately 3 centimetres (1 inch) apart. If you are a perfectionist you will go to great pains to measure out the seed exactly, but if you're like me, you'll sow them as thinly as possible and then thin them out if they come up too thickly. (You can use the thinnings for salads or quick steaming.) Once the seeds are in the ground, cover them lightly with soil, using the flat side of your rake to tamp the soil 57

down. Three or four rows about a metre (3 feet) in length and 13 centimetres (5 inches) apart should do just nicely for the first sowing.

Carrots are another crop that can be sown now, using virtually the
same technique. With carrots, sowing the seed very thinly cannot be
over-stressed, as the carrot root fly is attracted by the smell at the
thinning-out stage. I realize it is difficult to sow thinly, and if the carrot
root fly is really bad in your garden, I strongly recommend covering
carrots immediately after sowing with Reemay cloth. It is made out of
sunbonded polyester, which breathes and lets light and moisture
through while keeping the carrot root flies out. Keep the cloth on until
the carrots have reached maturity, only raising it for weeding or thinning. Some good early sweet carrots are 'Baby Finger Nantes' and 'Baby
Orange'.

Spinach, lettuce and radishes can be also be sown early. Space the
rows just a little wider apart than the width of your hoe blade.

In the flower department, there are a few bedding plants that can go
out early in the month, provided they have been properly hardened off.
They include snapdragons, stocks, and marguerite daisies. Seed for
bachelor buttons, shirley poppies, California poppies, and calendula
can be sown at the same time.

When planting out bedding plants, water them well the night before,
so that they slide out easily in a block from the basket. With an old
kitchen knife, cut them into individual blocks of soil, each with its own
plant. Don't try to pull the sections apart. Some plants will end up with
bare roots, while others will take all the soil.

A hand trowel is a good tool for planting out the bedding plants. Dig
the hole a little larger than the actual root ball. Try to keep the soil surface close to the level it was in the basket, then just fill in with soil
around the roots and firm it in lightly with your fingertips. It should be
firm enough that you can't pull the plant up easily. When you're finished, the plant should be in a slight depression rather than on a hill,
for ease of watering.

The spacing of plants depends on the type of plant, but as a general
rule of thumb, vegetables should be given more space than flowers. If
vegetables have to compete for soil nutrients, they sometimes go immediately to seed. Too close planting also cuts down on air circulation,

leading to prime conditions for fungus diseases to thrive.

Vegetables also need to be planted on time. They should never be allowed to become starved in their baskets, because once their growth cycle has been checked they go to seed. When selecting vegetables at your local nursery, make sure they are not yellow looking, or in the case of cabbages and cauliflowers, bluish purple. When I was a child, my father once gave me some leftover cauliflower plants for my garden. They were quite starved looking, and soon after I planted them they went straight to flower and formed little cauliflowers about 5 centimetres (2 inches) across!

Cabbages, cauliflowers and broccoli should be spaced 45 centimetres (18 inches) apart and brussels sprouts even further, about 60 centimetres (24 inches). This leaves a lot of bald space, but it can be utilized by sowing a crop of radishes in between, which will be ready for harvesting in a month's time, long before the cabbages fill the space.

Spring and Summer Bulbs

After your bulbs have put on their spring show and started to die back, the first step in their care and grooming is to remove the flower heads so that the plant doesn't waste energy forming seed.

Many people wonder when they can cut off the leaves of daffodils and tulips. Studies carried out at the Royal Horticultural Society's garden at Wisley in England a few years back recommended that the leaves should be left on for six weeks, which apparently allows the bulb to build up for the following season. Whatever you do, don't tie daffodil leaves in neat little knots. It simply cuts off the growing cycle and looks just too tidy for words!

Tulips and hyacinths are never as good in their second and third 59 years so they are best carefully lifted and moved to an area of the garden that doesn't matter as much. Tulips are always tricky to lift as the flower stems come from the base of the bulb rather than from the point at the top. Consequently they snap off right at the base, resulting in a leaf-producing bulb for at least the next couple of years.

To solve this problem I borrowed a technique from a fellow gardener. When planting bulbs in the fall, plant them in clumps in pots, then bury the pot. In late spring when they have finished blooming, simply lift the bulbs, pot and all, and move them to an area of the garden where they can die back naturally. Once the cycle has been completed, around mid-June, store them in a shed for replanting in another area of your garden next fall.

Daffodils and narcissi put on a good show for years when left in the same situation, and I have started planting the bulbs deeper than suggested, about one and a quarter trowels deep. When they've finished blooming, I plant my annuals—petunias, marigolds, and so on—in between the daffodils. Bedding plants don't usually require a hole larger than one trowel in depth, so the bulbs are undisturbed and as the annuals grow they hide the debris of the dying daffodil foliage.

We're getting to the time of year when summer-flowering bulbs and tubers should be planted—gladioli, freesias, dahlias, and the like. You may be surprised to find that freesias can be grown outside here. The 'Paradise' strain has been specifically developed for outdoor culture, but it is extremely important to have the right soil conditions. It must be well drained, with plenty of well-rotted manure worked into it.

Freesias also lend themselves to patio and balcony pots that are at least 30 centimentres deep by 30 wide (12 inches square). The bulbs should be planted fairly close together—3 centimetres (1¼ inches) apart and about the same depth—resulting in a pot full of exquisite and sweetly scented blooms in August.

Some of you may have started your dahlia tubers inside in pots to get a head start, and they can go out now. Dahlias like lots of room to grow. Plant them in holes a spade's depth by a spade's width and work bonemeal or well-rotted manure into the base of the hole. If the dahlias are newly purchased this year they'll only have one or two tubers, but if they're old established plants they'll be large clumps. The clumps can be separated carefully at this time, although I prefer to do mine in the fall when the stems and roots are soft and green.

Dahlias need good support, so when the shoots first show through the soil surface, push brushwood in all around them. It will look a bit odd to start with, but as the dahlias grow they'll hide the sticks. This works well with any perennial.

Balcony and Patio Gardens

If you have a sheltered south-facing patio, and you live in a mild area of the province, then you could well be able to plant up your patio containers by the beginning of May. Before you begin, however, you should be aware of some general principles of patio and balcony gardening.

The size of your pots is important. The minimum size, particularly if you don't want to be watering every hour during the height of the summer, is 30 centimetres (12 inches) cubed. Those large black nursery pots (the ones we used to refer to as five-gallon pots) are good because they hold moisture well and warm up earlier than other containers, allowing you to plant much earlier. (However, as mentioned elsewhere, when the sun is very hot, these pots must be shielded to protect the plants.)

Your containers can be constructed from any material that is durable for a season or more. Baskets lined with heavy black plastic make attractive containers. Recycled wooden packing boxes are fine as long as the wood has been treated with a preservative. (However, this has to be done at least six weeks previous to planting, to give the preservative time to be absorbed into the wood. Liquid preservative is toxic to plants.)

61

All containers that are out in the open and exposed to our sometimes long rains will need drainage holes. Without them containers can quickly turn into swamps. Drill the holes in the sides near the base of the pot, if the container is flat-bottomed. I do this with my half-barrel gardens. Of course, once you have drainage holes you need drainage trays to catch the excess water, if you live any higher than the ground floor in an apartment. Watering the downstairs neighbours when they are enjoying the sun is not the best way to meet them!

You will also need some drainage material in the bottom of the pot. Rocks are fine, although a little heavy. I use recycled styrofoam cups and crumple up the small plastic containers in which bedding plants are sold.

If you purchase ready-mixed potting soil, check its composition before adding fertilizer. Some mixes already have well-rotted manure added and you won't need to add granular fertilizer—in fact, you shouldn't add it, as overdoses of fertilizer can burn the roots of plants and kill them. Don't overfill your containers before adding the plants, because as you plant you will be adding soil. As always, leave at least 3 centimetres (1 inch) between the soil level and the rim of the pot, for watering.

When planting into containers, plant a little closer than you normally would in the garden. This will result in a vivid display of colour that can completely hide the pots. One year we had a wonderful summer display of annuals, including petunias, marigolds and flowering maples (*Abutilon*). Each pot was planted with one type of flower, then we massed them together at different levels, placing some at the back on upturned pots. The result was stunning by mid-summer, when all the pots were hidden by the plants, particularly the petunias. The bank of colour was as good as any you'd see in a show garden.

If you have had a patio garden for some time, you may well have bulbs in them right now. If they are daffodil or narcissi that have been planted deeply, you can probably leave them in the container and plant annuals right on top of them. But if they are tulip bulbs, I strongly recommend lifting them and giving them to a friend who has a garden, as they are never as good in their second season.

62 Many people are familiar with growing tomatoes or herbs in a bal-

cony garden, but have you every considered growing potatoes? You may think potatoes take up a lot of space in your garden, but if you just want a few for the unforgettable taste of steamed new potatoes, just dug from the garden, there is an ingenious method for growing them in a half-barrel.

Prepare your barrel as above with about 7 centimetres (3 inches) of drainage material, then add 15 centimetres (6 inches) of really good garden soil mixed with well-rotted compost or mushroom manure. Place four potatoes in a square, equally spaced, and cover them with a further 5 centimetres (2 inches) of soil. Each time the potatoes grow up through the surface, cover them with another 5-centimetre (2-inch) layer of soil, continuing until you reach within 7 centimetres (3 inches) of the barrel rim.

This may all seem rather strange, but there is logic behind it. Potatoes form off the stem, as opposed to the roots of the plant, so the more stem there is, the more potatoes can be produced. Provided the soil is good and rich, and you keep them well-watered, they should reward you with a crop in late June to early July. A good early variety to try is 'Early Warba'.

Vegetable Gardens— Planting out Warm Crops

Garden centres are carrying a wider range of vegetable plants for sale than ever before, showing a tendency away from concentrating exclusively on flowers. Even if you only have a small garden, you should try to grow a few vegetables, as there is nothing like home-grown flavour.

If you have a regular garden plot, by mid-May you will probably have   63 already planted out your peas, broad beans, lettuce, spinach and potatoes. If you haven't, there is still time to put most of these in. In the previous column, I covered a unique way of growing just a few potatoes. You can use the same method in your garden using old tires instead of a half-barrel. Start your potatoes out in a tire ring placed on the ground, making sure to put soil in the tire cavity as well. As the potatoes grow, cover them and add more tires up to a total of four.

If you live on the coast, it is usually safe to plant out tomatoes, squash, corn, peppers and all the other heat-loving vegetables by the end of May or thereabouts. To get a head start on your corn, you can sow some indoors in peat pots about mid-May.

First soak the seed for a couple of hours in a glass of water to soften the hard seed case. Then follow the same method as with peas and beans, keeping the seeds between layers of wet paper towelling until little roots appear. Sow them in pairs in small pots and keep them in a warm spot, out of direct sun, until it's warm enough to plant them in the garden—about two weeks.

Everyone will have their own favourite corn, but you should know that close to coastal waters, where there are cool sea breezes, it is better to choose a quick-maturing crop. Away from the water, just about any variety will do. Corn should, of course, be in a sunny spot, and you will get better results if you plant in blocks or clumps instead of rows. Corn needs to be pollinated in order to set seed (the tasty part that we like to eat). The pollen-producing flowers are the grass-like tops of the plant and when planted in rows, the wind carries most of the pollen away, instead of allowing it to be caught on the tassels of the forming cobs. I like to plant in clumps of nine plants, placed 45 centimetres (18 inches) apart in all directions. For a very sweet corn, try 'Illini Xtra Sweet'.

Tomatoes can usually go out the last week of May. If it's not yet time to plant out, but you have some tomatoes that are crying out to be planted, I would recommend potting them on to the next size pot. Just giving them this extra new soil will allow them to keep going without a check to their growth, but be very careful not to break up the rootball. When planting out, bury them just to the level of the two seed leaves and if they are top-heavy, support them with a stake or bamboo cane.

Tomatoes need a lot of warm days and nights to mature, and two of the best varieties for the cooler coastal areas are 'Celebrity' and 'Sweet 100s'.

All members of the curcubit family—that is squash, pumpkin and zucchini—enjoy well-rotted organic material at the roots, and often old-time gardeners grew them right on top of the compost heap. This had two advantages: not only did it provide plenty of nutrients for the roots, but the heat from the compost pile helped protect the plants early in the season.

You may not have a compost pile large enough to grow all the squash, pumpkin and zucchini you want, but you can build some mini compost piles right in the vegetable garden. One year we grew giant squash and pumpkins by using well-rotted leaf-mould from leaves that had been composted for two seasons.

To make your beds, make a hole at least 60 centimetres (2 feet) across and 30 centimetres (1 foot) deep for each plant. Fill the holes with leaf-mould, well-rotted manure, or compost, then pile some of the excess soil on top and up the sides. Once the mound is complete, firm it down lightly with your foot and make a slight indentation in the top. Mix 15 millilitres (1 tablespoon) of superphosphate lightly in each hole before placing the plants, one on the top of each mound. The super-phosphate will promote rapid root development and as soon as the roots hit the organic matter, you're well on your way to growing the best squash in the neighborhood or a pumpkin large enough to enter the world pumpkin festival weigh-in at VanDusen Gardens.

It is best to wait for the first week of June to plant curcubits, but if you have to do it early, bend some heavy wire into hoops over the plants (two hoops per plant) and cover with clear plastic to form little tents. Bury the edges in the soil to prevent the wind from blowing them away. These mini-tents are operated just like a cold frame: open them on sunny days and close them one hour before sundown. Cucumbers will also appreciate the warmth, being related to pumpkin and squash, and they enjoy plenty of organic material in the soil.

I like to train my cucumbers onto a trellis. Plant your cucumber plants in a row about 30 centimetres (12 inches) apart, then place the trellis at about a forty-five degree slant away from the plants, anchoring it with some small posts or stakes. Our trellis is one metre (3 feet)   65 square and the outside frame is constructed of 10- by 5-centimetre (4- by 2-inch) lumber. The crisscross forming the trellis is made from 5-centimetre (2-inch) slats. Throughout the growing season, you'll have to train the cucumbers to grow onto and all over the trellis, but when the cucumbers form, they hang down through the trellis, where they are easy to harvest and nice and clean.

Peppers need to be planted in the warmest and sunniest part of your garden in well-drained soil; they need at least ten hours of sun a day to be successful. Plant them 30 centimetres (12 inches) apart in staggered double rows. We have had success with a delicious yellow pepper called 'Early Sweet Banana' which produced many 15-centimetre-long (6-inch) fruits.

Last but not least, don't forget to sow some beans. Pole beans make a wonderful quick-growing privacy screen for the summer, and are not only ornamental but give you delicious beans to eat later on in the summer. Soak them first, as with all members of the bean and pea family, and plant them when the new shoots are just beginning to show. 'Scarlet Runner' is a popular old favourite and 'Provider' is one of my favourite bush beans.

Planting for Colour

Towards the end of May, it's time to get all your annual bedding plants in and there is always a wonderful array of colour in the garden centres.

I have always been a stickler for planting colours that complement each other in the garden, but I'm well aware that it is a very personal thing. In nature, when wild flowers grow together, it seems that every colour harmonizes with every other colour. However, where I was trained in horticulture in the UK, we had a long annual border, 24 metres (78 feet) wide by 2 metres (6 feet) deep, and it was planted starting with white at one end, going through yellow to orange to red to purple to blue. It was certainly eye-catching.

If you think it might be fun to try, it's easily possible to achieve that sort of effect in the home garden.

Starting with white, sweet alyssum is quite widely sold as an edging plant, as it is short and highly perfumed, as the name implies. Viola 'White Perfection' is a little taller and very showy. Annual gypsophila reaches about 45 centimetres (18 inches) in height and is beautifully light and airy. A must for the home garden is nicotiana, or tobacco plant, which spreads its sweet scent over the garden on warm summer evenings. 'Niki White' is an erect nicotiana that grows up to a metre (3 feet) in height.

Any of the marigolds would qualify for the yellow section. The shorter ones stand up better to wet weather and can be used as a border. The annual calceolaria is much smaller-flowered than the houseplant variety, but still has attractive balloon-like flowers. For a climbing yellow vine, try canary creeper. It is related to the nasturtium, but has numerous smaller showy blossoms. Gloriosa daisies are in their prime mid to late summer and are superb as cut flowers for the house.

When it comes to orange, again there are marigolds, but don't forget orange zinnias, California poppies and cosmos 'Bright Lights'.

Reds include salvias, which have been hybridized recently to be more compact and manageable; New Guinea impatiens, which tolerates the sun and usually has dark red foliage as well; and some very fine verbenas, such as 'Showtime Blaze'.

Purples include heliotrope, which we used to call cherry pie because that's exactly what it smells like right after a summer shower, and larkspur, which is really an annual delphinium. Blue is my favourite colour in my own garden. Try sowing nigella, or love-in-a-mist, from seed—it's quite easy—or buy it as a bedding plant. Bachelor's buttons are an old favourite and there is a beautiful African daisy, *Felicia amelloides*, sometimes sold as blue marguerite. It isn't grown as widely as it should be, but if you see it, do give it garden space. You won't be disappointed. *Phacelia campanularia*, the California bluebell, likes a good sunny spot and is the most brilliant of blues.

When planting your annual border, try to have the soil well worked with some mushroom manure forked into the top 15 centimetres (6 inches) or so. Directly before planting add some granular 6-8-6 at a handful per square metre (square yard). If the soil is moist, stand or kneel on a board so that the soil doesn't get too compacted. And please don't plant annuals in a straight row; they are not vegetables. Plant them fairly close together–a trowel's length apart for very short-growing plants, a trowel and a half for plants in the 45-centimetre (18-inch) range, and two trowels for the tallest.

When it comes to the balcony and patio garden, you can achieve a similar effect with containers. I usually try to stick to one colour per container. A nice arrangement can be made with three containers of different heights—perhaps with white marguerites in the top one, red geraniums in the middle and blue lobelia in the shortest one.

But be sure not to forget the edibles in your patio garden, many of which have been mentioned already, such as potatoes and tomatoes. For a change, try some rhubarb chard. It is most attractive and delicious, and you can harvest just a few leaves now and then so that the plant is always there for effect. The brilliant red stems look superb with the sun shining through them. By all means experiment and enjoy— both with colour and flavour!

Lawns and Ground Covers

Throughout most of our province the soil is on the acidic side, and the continual use of lawn foods such as 10-6-4 to get the greenest lawn on the block only adds to the problem of overgrowth of moss. If you haven't fed your lawn yet and it is showing signs of weaker growth and perhaps yellowing, feed it with any balanced fertilizer, such as my favourite 6-8-6 at a handful per square metre (square yard). Just sprinkle it on and if the weather is dry, water it in.

High first numbers are for leaf and stem growth and thus provide that quick green everyone is looking for, but the most important number is the middle one, as it is phosphate and promotes good root development. The last number is potash, which promotes general health and flowering and fruiting. If anything, you want to discourage seed heads from appearing in your lawn.

I recommend feeding at this time of year, again in late July, and once more at the beginning of September. With that last feeding, it is even more important that the first number be low, as you don't want new tender grass to develop before the frost.

When it comes to weeds in the lawn, I balk at using fertilizer that has herbicide added to it. First of all, it is a waste to spread herbicide over the whole lawn if the weeds are in isolated patches. If they are sporadic broad-leafed weeds like dandelion or plantain, then I am a great believer in getting out there with an old kitchen knife and cutting them off below ground level. I know dandelions will grow again from a cut root, so try to go as deep as possible without wrecking the lawn.

With other tiresome weeds like clover, English daisies and creeping trefoil, I prefer to spot treat them with something like Later's Weed-Be-Gone. It comes premixed in a convenient spray bottle and is best applied after a warm rain when the weeds are actively growing. You have to be persistent, applying it perhaps twice a week, until the weeds have succumbed. If you have children or pets, keep the area being treated wired off with chicken wire or something similar, just to be on the safe side.

Having said "tiresome English daisies," I should clarify that I quite like seeing them in lawns. But that is all a matter of choice, as some people like a smooth, pure-green expanse of lawn.

Older lawns can suffer badly from moss infestation, particularly after a mild winter. Moss loves moist climates and acidic soils, both of which prevail in our area, where moss was resident long before human habitation. If a lot of high-nitrogen fertilizers are added over the years, it can create so much acidity in the soil that the lawn will just die out and the moss will take over totally.

If you have a very old lawn that is predominantly mossy and you can afford to redo it, it might not be a bad idea to totally redo the lawn by turning it under and adding some good topsoil (organic material like mushroom manure or well-rotted manure, and perhaps some sand if the drainage isn't good). If you decide to take this drastic action, plan to do it in March or September.

If your lawn is about 50 percent moss, try raking it. For a large lawn, you can rent a power rake from your local garden centre. The moss you cull from the lawn can be composted, and be sure to save some of the nice-looking bits for lining your hanging baskets.

After raking, the next step is to spike, or aerate, the lawn, and this should be done in April. Here again, commercial spikers are available to rent for large areas. If you have the time or need the exercise, go over the lawn with a garden fork, sticking it into the lawn about every 15 centimetres (6 inches), to a depth of 7 centimetres (3 inches). This prepares the lawn for the addition of new soil to the root area.

The top dressing can be a good mixture of soil, like potting mix or some screened mushroom manure. It is lightly sprinkled over the lawn, then raked or brushed into the holes. A healthy lawn needs a strong root system, and phosphate is the element used by plants for developing their roots, so at the brushing-in stage sprinkle a handful of super-phosphate for every square metre (square yard) of lawn. The lawn should then be fertilized regularly, as suggested above. A balanced fertilizer like 4-10-10 or 6-8-6 will build up the root system and boost the health of the grass plants themselves. If the plants are thick enough, they will be too dense for moss to penetrate.

People seem to hate moss with a passion, but if your lawn just doesn't thrive, there are some alternatives. If you've tried everything and you still seem to be losing the battle with moss in your lawn, consider taking the opposite approach and cultivating a moss lawn, like those in Japanese gardens. Admittedly it won't stand much continuous traffic, or activities like ball games, but it can look extremely attractive. The Japanese Garden at UBC and the Meditation Garden at the VanDusen Botanical Gardens are two good examples of how moss can be used to advantage in a landscape, giving a pleasing, soft green ground cover year round that doesn't need mowing.

There are a variety of other ground covers that can effectively take the place of lawn. Although they are not hardy for continuous heavy traffic, if paths are placed through high-traffic areas, a ground cover can be visually pleasing. Creeping thyme works well, provided there is plenty of sun and the soil is well drained. When it is walked on the aroma is delightful. It flowers profusely with purple flowers early in the summer.

Before planting, prepare the soil well by adding some organic matter. The thyme can be planted in April or May—every 15 centimetres (6 inches) if they are small plants, 30 centimetres (12 inches) if they are larger. It won't be long until they are all touching.

For those difficult shaded areas, such as under large trees, where grass will never grow well, try planting periwinkle. Some people think it is a weedy plant, but if used properly it can be most effective when covered with bright blue blossoms in late spring. When planting under trees, use well-established plants from 15-centimetre (6-inch) pots and add some good soil around each planting hole to get them established quickly in the first season. Above all, keep them well watered.

Two plants from the UBC Botanical Gardens are hard to beat as ground covers. The first is a form of a native B.C. plant commonly called kinikinik by the native peoples. Another name is bearberry, simply because the bears love to eat it in the fall. This strain is called *Arctostaphylos* 'Vancouver Jade' because of its jade green foliage. It grows fast and has an abundance of pretty pink flowers that are held above the foliage and are therefore quite showy in May. It thrives in sun or shade and can tolerate well-drained soils.

The other one is a *Rubus*, or a relative of blackberries and raspberries. It was collected at high elevations in Taiwan and has proved to be very hardy in B.C. It has tiny ruffled emerald-green leaves along low tough branches that hug the ground—thus its name, *Rubus* 'Emerald Carpet.' I like it because it does well in shady areas, even under the shade of cedar trees, which, as you know, can be quite difficult to deal with.

If you want to boost quick growth of these ground covers, give the area a top dressing of good soil and some well-rotted compost or leaf-mould before planting. Plant small plants from 10-centimetre (4-inch) 71 pots about 45 centimetres (18 inches) apart and keep them well watered the first year. After that, just keep them in trim by cutting the edges with hedging shears.

Bugs and Pests

Finally your garden is planted and everything is thriving. Unfortunately, the conditions that make your garden grow also promote weed growth. And the tender new shoots that are coming up look like dinner to a wide variety of pests and bugs. Each year they return, and sometimes with a vengeance: caterpillars, aphids, cutworms and others. If you want to protect your garden without having an entire arsenal of poisonous pesticides, there are some solutions.

Tent caterpillars are a problem every year and there really is no easy way to get rid of them, especially when they are near the top of a very large tree. If you can reach them with pruners, then cut the infected branch out and either step on or burn the caterpillars. Later on in the year, when the rather fat brown moths are around, try to watch out for their egg clusters. They are laid in largish 3-centimetre (1-inch) clusters resembling brown styrofoam that surround young branches. When you see them, scrape them off the tree. A handout from the BC Wildlife Rescue Association, about alternate pesticides, notes that if hot peppers are ground up in water and sprayed on the caterpillars they will die. Or try dusting cayenne pepper onto the clusters of caterpillars early in the morning while there is still dew on the foliage.

Weevils can also be a problem. They are those snout-nosed little slow-moving beetles that sometimes get in through a door or window and often lie on their backs with their legs waving in the air. At that stage, of course, they seem harmless and are easy to catch. But if you go out into your garden at night with a flashlight and check the rhododendrons and plants like strawberries, you would find dozens of them actively chewing neat little circular bites all around the edges of the leaves.

If your rhododendron is single-stemmed, with none of the outer branches touching the soil, then paint the trunk with "tree tangle foot," an old product used years ago on the trunks of fruit trees to trap coddling moths as they crawled up the trunk. It also traps weevils, but if they are on low-growing plants like strawberries, the only alternative to granular Diazinon is picking them off by hand at night.

Cutworms also come out at night. Again, they can be handpicked (easier to do if you wear gloves). Napthalene crystals or crushed mothballs worked into the soil surface at a handful per square metre (square yard) will keep them away, but in really bad infestations, Sevin is the recommended pesticide. It is a powder that is dusted on the plants.

This is the time of year when aphids start to become a plague. If you have rhubarb in your garden, collect 1½ kilograms (three pounds) of the leaves and boil them in 3 litres (quarts) of water. Cool and strain, then add a further litre (quart) of water with some true soap flakes mixed in it, and spray your plants. The aphids will drop off right before your eyes. Don't get carried away with this and add extra rhubarb leaves, though. Too many can burn or defoliate your plants. This concoction also controls wooly aphid, caterpillars and other biting insects. Remember that it is dangerous if ingested, so keep well out of the reach of children.

Slugs are the pests that everyone loves to hate. They prey on young seedlings, and it's not just the big slugs that do the damage. It's the tiny ones that hide so well in the garden by day, and then can eat a whole row of tiny, tasty new seedlings overnight. Again, handpicking by night can control them, but the old story about shaking salt on them really works. Better yet, if you live close to the sea, collect seaweed and put it all around your vegetable patch and in between the rows. Slugs won't crawl over freshly gathered seaweed for several weeks, because of the salt content. Eventually, when the seaweed rots, it adds nutrients to the soil for future crops.

Another method that can be very effective is homemade slug jails, using recycled plastic margarine or yogurt containers with lids. Cut three or four little holes on the side of the container near the base, so 73 that when it sits in the garden, the entrances are at slug level. Then put some bran-type slug bait in the bottom of the container, in a little pile in the centre, and carefully place the lid on. Set them around your newly planted garden. The lid prevents pets from eating the bait and keeps the bait dry. And, not least important, once the container is full of dead slugs, it can be thrown out with the garbage.

Fungus Diseases

Many areas of British Columbia are in almost rainforest micro-climates, which can lead to problems in the garden, such as moss, lichen and fungus. For quite a few years now our provincial emblem tree, the native dogwood, has been severely hit by a fungus disease known as dogwood blotch, for which there is no known cure.

For that particular disease and many other related fungus diseases, a long cool spring can create ideal conditions for rapid growth. A fungus called brown rot that attacks both ornamental and fruiting cherries has almost completely defoliated these trees in recent years. It occurs immediately after flowering and starts as a grey mould within the flower cluster. Eventually it kills the whole cluster, turning it brown.

Some of the earlier winter-flowering *Prunus autumnalis* can appear to be almost dead by spring. Unfortunately there is not much you can do. According to the provincial government's pest control for the home and garden, this is not the time of year to control it. They recommend Benomyl or Captan, both of which are fungicides to be sprayed at the pink bud stage. The pink bud stage is just before the flowers open.

If your tree is not too badly infected, it is probably a good idea to prune out the badly infected branches. For serious problems, it would mean cutting down the whole tree. Before you get carried away, you should know that it is possible that the tree can survive if the summer season is long and hot. If some leaves have survived, keep the tree well watered and feed it on a regular basis with liquid fish fertilizer. Later in the fall, just after leaf drop, rake up as many of the leaves as possible and put them out with the garbage or burn them. Then spray the tree with lime sulphur at 100 millilitres (2 cups) per litre (quart) of water. Apply it on a dry day and repeat a week to ten days later.

The same methods can apply to leaf blotch on dogwoods, or you could adopt a regular spraying program with benomyl at 1 millilitre per litre (¼ teaspoon per quart) every fourteen days. This is really only practical on newly planted trees, those under 4 metres (13 feet) in height.

Even the hardy rhubarb can be affected by bacterial disease, which causes overall weakening of the plant; the leaves are much smaller and the stalks are floppy and lie along the ground. Close examination of the plant ` ill reveal a brown rotting of the crown, often initially started by some damage to the plant. Unfortunately there is no cure for this condition and most of the books recommend digging up and discarding the plant. I would caution against taking what appear to be healthy side shoots from such a plant to start up new plants, as once the bacteria is present, it can spread. If you're planting new rhubarb, select a new location to avoid any risk of infection.

Raspberry rust seems to be quite widespread throughout the lower mainland some years. It occurs as little rust-like spots on the undersides of the leaves. For organic control, try 5 millilitres of epsom salts in a litre (1 teaspoon per quart) of water. Experiment at first by just spraying a few leaves. If it burns them, add more water.

The ever present problem of mildew on apple trees shows up in the distorted development of new foliage and premature dropping of leaves. If you have ornamental crab trees, you will be familiar with the constant dropping of brown leaves all summer long. Winter dormant sprays of lime sulphur are supposed to control this, but they don't, and there is little to be done about it by this time of year. The books recommend spraying a fungicide every fourteen days, but if you do and your neighbor doesn't, it is a waste of time.

I am not a lover of using fungicides or pesticides, and there really isn't such a thing as an organic fungicide, unless you count sulphur,   75 which is mined. Sulphur can be used quite effectively on smaller plant fungus diseases such as mildew on begonias. To apply it you need a duster and there are some small hand-held models on the market with a screw-top lid. The dry sulphur is placed inside the cannister and a spout ensures even coverage.

J U N E

CHAPTER SIX

Water Gardens

Water can be a lovely addition to a garden landscape. One of the nicest water features in a public garden is at VanDusen Gardens, where the lakes are filled with superb collections of water lilies and edged with all kinds of fascinating bog plants.

But you don't have to have a lake to incorporate water very nicely into your own home garden, and the presence of water can have a very soothing and calming effect. Although ponds have had some bad publicity because of possible accidents, there are precautions that can be taken to make them more safe.

You can make your own pond by digging a hole and lining it with a strong heavy-gauge plastic or some similar manufactured material, or you may want to purchase a prefabricated fibreglass pool from a specialized garden centre or through Moore Water Gardens, Port Stanley, Ontario, N0L 2A0. Their catalogue is fascinating as it has such a large selection of water lilies to choose from.

If you want lilies, keep that in mind from the beginning stages of planning your pool. Choose an open spot with good sunlight, as they need sun to bloom, and remember that lilies need to have the correct 77 water depth. There should be at least 15 and preferably 30 centimetres (6 to 12 inches) of water above the crown of the plant. However, for most lilies it should not be more than 38 centimetres (15 inches). Excavating to a depth of 60 centimetres (24 inches) should leave enough room for adequate container size and the optimum depth.

The best time to be planting lilies is right through to the end of this month. You will need 30-centimetre (12-inch) containers, either wooden or clay pots, with drainage holes in the bottom.

Lilies like a good rich top soil. In the old days we used to add quite a bit of well-rotted manure to it, but this is frowned on now as it discolours the water and makes it smelly. When you get your Moores catalogue, you will notice that there are special fertilizer pellets available made from organic material. It is not recommended to use inorganic fertilizers like 6-8-6 as they can be quite harmful to lily roots.

Plant the lily so that the crown is flush with the soil surface, leaving at least 5 centimetres (2 inches) between the soil surface and the rim of the container. You can then fill this space up with gravel, which prevents soil from floating out and stops fish from disturbing the soil and clouding the pool.

Have your pond filled well in advance so that the water has a chance to warm up, and then lower the lilies gently into place. I have to smile when I remember one of my very first jobs at horticultural college—draining a pool and dividing some clumps of well-established water lilies. What a smelly and muddy job it was! But gently lowering newly planted lilies into a new pond is another thing altogether.

Marginal planting—along the shore—is something else to think about. Cattails, marsh marigolds and water iris are very attractive. They all like soil similar to that of lilies and need their feet in the water all the time. Plant them exactly as you would water lilies and stand the pots around the edge of the pond on rocks or blocks. If the ground right next to the pond's edge is swampy, plant some primulas or other moist-soil-loving plants.

People who live in townhouses and apartments can also enjoy water gardens. Barrels, cut to the appropriate height for water lilies, make fine containers, and on checking through a catalogue, you will find that there are some lilies that prefer shallower water. I have also seen a very nice pool built up from a townhouse patio. It was 60 centimetres (2 feet) high and about 2 metres (6 feet) square. All around the edge was a ledge wide enough to sit on, so that one could watch the fish and gaze at the lilies when they were in bloom. A nice extra touch was an electric circulating pump, so that a fountain could be turned on.

Even if you aren't planning to put in a pool at this time, consider it as a fall or winter project. If you're worried about safety, strong open nylon netting can be stretched taut across the surface of the pool just below the water surface. It is not very noticeable and can save a child from drowning. It also prevents herons and raccoons from stealing your fish. Incidentally, having fish in a pool will keep the mosquito larvae eaten, reducing the mosquito problem.

Weed, Feed, and Water

Towards the end of June, fine sunny weather really comes into its own here in B.C. and the gardens start to take off. Unfortunately, so do the weeds.

Weeding is an ongoing activity that will probably be around until the end of time, but careful winter planning and cultivation can certainly cut down on the amount of weeds occurring in the garden. If you have the problem right now, though, there are a few things to know.

Sunny weather is the right time to weed, as you can leave the weeds lying on the surface of the soil to shrivel and die in the sun (a comforting thought for any gardener). Hoeing is still one of the best ways to eliminate seedling weeds. The traditional Dutch hoe, or push hoe, is the best tool for the job, as it allows you to walk backwards between rows, gently disturbing the top centimetre (½ inch) of soil with a short, sharp pushing motion. Don't go any deeper than that as it will disturb the surface feeder roots of your plants and that can lead to crop damage. Beware of electrical and mechanical weeders, as they appear to bite too deeply into the earth.

A swoe is a hoe with a cutting edge on both the front and back, which enables the user to cut weeds with both a push and pull action.

My old head gardener always believed in hoeing at least once a week during the growing season even if the weeds weren't showing. It's a good idea, as the constant moving of the soil doesn't allow the weeds to germinate.

Hoeing doesn't eliminate weeding altogether, but a little hand weeding after a hard day's work at the office can be very therapeutic. Looking ahead to next season, make a note in your logbook to dig any visible weeds under by turning the soil one spade's depth in November. The burying will turn any growing weeds into compost and can cut down significantly on the weeds that grow next year.

Perennial weeds are the ones that cause so much grief as it's almost impossible to eradicate them. Some examples in this category are morning glory, goutweed and buttercups. Pulling them up can compound the problem, as it causes the underground roots to divide and produce more of the same. You might have to resort to using a contact killer like Amitrole T. It must be applied carefully to leaf and stem surfaces using something like a paintbrush. Be sure to wear rubber gloves and remember that it will kill any plant with which it comes in contact.

The second main task as spring moves into summer is to keep the garden well watered. This is particularly true of the vegetable garden, simply because many food plants will go straight to seed if they dry out during their critical development stage.

Watering is best done in the morning before it gets too hot. This is because evening watering can create ideal conditions for fungus disease growth—high humidity plus cooler night temperatures. This is particularly true of peas, cucumbers, and zucchinis, which are susceptible to powdery mildew. Don't water during the heat of the day, since theoretically the water droplets on the plants can magnify the heat of the sun and burn the leaves. However, don't carry this to extremes—if you see a poor little plant wilting in the heat of the day around noon, don't wait until evening to give it water! Just try to get the water to the soil area and not on the leaves.

The next thing to remember when hand watering is to give the plants enough to be useful. Don't just damp the surface of the soil; it's much better to thoroughly soak the soil once or twice a week than to damp it down daily.

A 5-centimetre (2-inch) layer of mulch will help both to eliminate weeds and retain moisture. Grass clippings are fine to mulch with if the lawn has not been treated with one of those fertilizers that have broad-leaf weed killers added to it. The herbicide can build up and cause many problems for your garden plants.

The exception to mulching in the garden is rhododendrons. They can stand a small layer of mulch, but their surface roots are very important, and if covered too deeply, it can inhibit their flowering.

With container gardening, it is crucial to water hanging baskets and patio pots once a day, or even twice if the pots are smaller or if they are exposed to wind. This constant watering leaches out the food value in the soil, so a program of feeding is essential if you want your baskets to be attractive right into the fall.

With hanging baskets, it is quite safe to feed every time you water, with one of the water-soluble fertilizers, like 20-20-20 or liquid fish fertilizer. When you are feeding every day, you must dilute the recommended amount by half, to avoid burning the plants. Larger patio containers need only be fed once or twice a week, at the regular strength.

Between Seasons

June is always a bit of a doldrum time—in between the great splash of spring colour and waiting for the summer show to happen. It can be a good time to sit back and assess your garden, perhaps planning for next year, to do a little garden maintenance, and—surprising as it sounds—sow seed for next spring's pansies, wallflowers and primroses.

Many people forget about fall bedding plants, but in mild coastal climates they do very well. You need a small area for a seed sowing bed, which will be prepared as for all seed sowing, adding granular phosphate at a handful per square metre (square yard). Make your rows 15 centimetres (6 inches) apart and keep in mind that the amount of seedlings that germinate in 30 centimetres (12 inches) of row will provide enough plants for most home gardeners.

In a few weeks, around mid-July, they'll be large enough for transplanting into any spare spots you can find in the garden. Allow them about 17 centimetres (7 inches) of space all around so that they can develop into large healthy plants. There they'll thrive in the summer sun until it's time to plant them into their beds (late September or early October—the same time you'll put your bulbs in).

If your so-called winter pansies have come through the winter with flying colours, you may have wondered whether or not you should take them out. I vote for leaving them in. As long as you keep the deadheads picked off, the blossoms will keep coming, so just plant your summer annuals around them. Even if your pansies overwintered well, though, you should be resowing them at this time.

Some annuals, like snapdragons, not only survive a mild winter, but start to produce many blossoms about now. Here again, there is no need to take out these overwintering annuals. In fact, in slightly more temperate areas, snapdragons form shrub-like plants that survive for a number of years.

If you have a little patch of bare soil, about one metre (3 feet) square, and want to try sowing some seed for a winter or early spring vegetable garden, sow a few rows of cauliflower, broccoli, or curly kale. Prepare your soil as usual, by forking it over and removing weeds and rocks. Sprinkle on some 6-8-6 and rake it in when you level the soil.

Make your drills about 5 millimetres (¼ inch) deep, and 15 centimetres (6 inches) apart. When the seed has germinated and the seedlings are large enough to handle, transplant them into areas of your garden where the early summer crops like peas are ready for pulling out. This way you'll be all set for greens, and in good time.

Now is the time to store those bulbs you lifted out in the spring. If you heeled them into the ground, it may be hard to remember where they are, but there should still be a few dead leaves showing to mark the spot. Try to choose a sunny day to lift them, so that after you've cleaned them off they can dry in the sun for awhile before they are stored somewhere with good air circulation. When you're lifting the bulbs, cull the small ones, as they simply won't produce flowers next season. If you have the space, plant them in a spare area of the garden, such as a shrub bed, to grow on to flowering size in a few years time.

Apart from roses and perhaps some flag iris, there is very little in bloom in the June garden, and it may even be looking a little dull. It isn't the right time for planting, but it is a perfect time to make some notes for next fall or spring on how you'd like to change your garden.

A plant that I can recommend for brightening up the garden is a vine, closely related to the kiwi fruit, called *Actinidia kolmikta*. It well deserves its common name of painted kiwi, for the newly developed leaves look exactly as though they have pink paint splashed all over them. The leaves are about 15 centimetres (6 inches) long and 10 centimetres (4 inches) wide and the vine also flowers. It looks very attractive growing up an old cedar tree stump, or even up a cedar tree, as the dark background really shows off the foliage.

Pyrethrum daisy, a perennial chrysanthemum that is often sold under the name of painted daisy, is another attractive plant that gives good colour at this time of year. There are several named cultivars; 'Brenda' is a really good dark pink. They are ideal for a border but do need supporting. Once they have finished flowering, cut them back almost to ground level and they'll send up a second growth of flower stems. You may recognize the species name of this daisy, as an extract from the plant is used as an organic pest control.

Flag iris, mentioned above, is worth investigating as a group. They come in a wide range of colours, from bronzes and yellows through pink and magenta to the darkest of purples. Their botanical name is *Iris germanica*, simply because the plant was first discovered in Germany. They aren't as popular as they could be because of their short blooming period, but they do give a wonderful show in June.

The best time to transplant iris is in the fall. You will find that they have a rhizome running along the surface of the soil. Never bury the rhizome when planting; in order to produce good flowers each season, it needs to be at the soil surface where it can have sunshine.

An unusual June flowering tree is *Stewartia pseudocamellia*. As the name implies, the flowers resemble those of the camellia, except that they are white. This tree is an ideal candidate for the small garden. It is slow-growing, although it can eventually reach 17 metres (65 feet). Best of all, the small leaves are beautifully coloured in the fall, and they are followed by attractive dark brown seed pods in the winter, so the tree gives interest year-round in your garden.

There are some wonderful Asian primulas that bloom well into June, especially when planted in the shade of shrubbery. If you've got a shady spot that tends to be wet for most of the year, you must try these primulas, sometimes referred to as pagoda primroses, as the flowers occur in regular whorls at intervals up the flowering spike. Colours range from white and pale pink to oranges and dark red.

Of course, there are many other June-blooming plants, so get out your notebook and tour your local parks and gardens at this time. You can get a lot of gardening ideas for next year.

Putting Houseplants out for the Summer

Many people put their houseplants outside for the summer, and there are many houseplants that love it and actually bloom better as a result of the change. However, it isn't a good common practice for all houseplants, as so many of them are native to tropical areas of the world that never experience nights as cool as those in B.C.

Many orchids need to be out for the summer. A more common species, cymbidium, is native to the cooler slopes of the Himalayas just below the snowline and it really appreciates some cooler nights. When I first came to UBC, there were some orchids that had been kept in the hottest greenhouse all their lives and had never bloomed. I learned about putting them outdoors from a friend in the Orchid Society, and the following winter they all sent up flower spikes.

Cymbidiums will want full sun all day, but when you first put them out, introduce them to the sun gradually.

Some plants that fall into the cactus group also love to spend the summer outdoors. The epiphyllum, or orchid cactus, and the Christmas cactus both have their origins in the jungles of South America, where they go through periods of rain and drought as well as drastic temperature changes. They both do well in an area where they get full morning sun followed by afternoon shade.

The so-called indoor-outdoor plants—hibiscus, flowering maple, lantana, and tibouchina, for example—work beautifully for patios and decks. Those who have greenhouses can overwinter them as trees, just like the Parks Board does, putting them out each summer. An important thing to remember is that although these plants come from areas with many hours of hot sun, once they have spent a winter in B.C., they are not used to sunshine. Just like us, they will burn easily if over-exposed. For their first days out, keep them shaded or semi-shaded, gradually introducing them to the sun over a week or so.

If you have had some of these plants for awhile, chances are they are quite potbound. If they must stay in the same size pot because it is the largest feasible size, then be sure to feed them with 20-20-20 or liquid fish fertilizer. As an alternative, they may be planted out in the summer. They will put out a great new root system that will nourish the plant. In the fall when you take it in, you will have to prune away excess root and top to make it fit into its overwintering pot again.

Plants that should not be put out for the summer include Norfolk Island pine, weeping fig, gardenia, philodendron and many more that are tropical. (However, I believe that the relationship between plants and people is very personal, and if you've been putting your gardenia out every summer and it's thrived, then by all means continue to do it!)

There are many houseplants that were never tropical, some examples being piggyback plant, ivy and strawberry begonia. These plants will probably all do much better outside in a cool location than they did all winter indoors.

One last point: once plants are outside for the summer they'll be susceptible to all the garden pests. Keep a sharp lookout in the fall when it's time to bring them back in—you don't want to bring all the pests in with them.

Rose Care

June is traditionally rose month, the time of the year when roses really come into their own and all the work pays off. To help them keep blooming as long as possible and to get the best possible show, there are a few things you can be doing, even this month.

If you didn't top dress them earlier, do it now, using some well-rotted manure or compost to a depth of 8 centimetres (3 inches). It will provide food and keep moisture in the ground during dry spells.

As the flowers finish blooming, remove the deadheads. If you have many multi-headed roses, such as polyantha or floribunda, deadheading becomes a daily chore, but few gardening tasks are as pleasantly scented. If they are multi-headed stems, cut the stem back to within two or three leaves of the main stem when the last bloom is spent. This will promote new growth from the base, giving more blooms midsummer to early September. The same holds true for single stemmed hybrid tea roses and climbers. For all roses, try to make the cut above an outward-facing leaf joint.

Roses are susceptible to insect pests, particularly aphids, which love to cluster on the succulent new rose shoots. If you're not squeamish, rub them off with your thumb and forefinger and squash them—or wear rubber gloves for this operation. Safers Insecticidal Soap works well if it is used frequently enough and directions are followed exactly. Another method is to make your own organic insecticide with rhubarb leaves (for directions, see page 73).

Fungus diseases like black spot and powdery mildew are not as easy to control, and your roses will be more susceptible if they are in an area with little air circulation. Black spot looks just like the name implies. Try to pick off any infected leaves as they appear and be careful not to let them drop back into the soil. The spores can overwinter and reinfect the bush next year. If black spot is bad, make a note in your logbook to spray them during December or January with the dormant spray of lime sulphur that is applied to fruit trees.

Powdery mildew is difficult to control once established. It looks a bit like chalk dust on the surface of the leaf. It is particularly bad on white roses and some of the old-fashioned ramblers like 'Dorothy Perkins'. All I can suggest is regular spraying with one of the recommended fungicides available at your garden centre. When mixing it, always add some pure soapflakes to the water. This will make it more effective as it will coat the unaffected leaf areas and prevent the spread of the disease.

Apart from regular watering (best done in the morning and directed onto the roots, avoiding the foliage) and a few caretaking chores, most of the month of June should be devoted to enjoying the heavenly scent and beautiful blooms of your roses. If you like to make your own gifts, the petals can be dried to make potpourri later on. Spread them out in a thin layer on a flat surface, amd dry them away from direct sun in an airy place like a carport or shed. When they are thoroughly dry, store them in a dry place until needed.

J U L Y

CHAPTER SEVEN

The Vegetable Patch—
Replacement Vegetables

Part of the fun of gardening is watching the constantly changing cycles of growth. Some of your vegetables will have completely finished producing by now, while others, the heat-loving vegetables, are just starting to look good.

Tomatoes need careful care and maintenance throughout their growing season, and at this stage they should be well staked and tied. When tying them, secure your twine around the stake before actually taking in the stem, so that it won't slip around and cause future problems. Make sure not to tie it too tightly, leaving room for the stem to fatten up.

Most tomatoes other than the bush type produce more abundantly if they are kept to a single stem. To do this, remove any side shoots as soon as they appear. The side shoots always occur at the leaf joints, or nodes, and they look like miniature tomato plants, while the fruit-producing clusters come from the main stem, on the part between two leaves. (In gardening language this is known as the internode.)

Don't be frightened to take the side shoots off, thinking that you may

destroy potential fruit. This is not where the fruit is produced. If you remove the shoots, the plant's energy will go into producing fruit rather than leaves. Even if the shoots have developed and are quite large, just prune them carefully with your pruning shears.

Some of the early-finishing crops will be dying back about now, freeing some garden space for new plantings. At this time you can renew your quick-growing vegetables, such as lettuce or radish, or if you sowed seed for a winter vegetable garden last month, the seedlings should be ready for transplanting. If you didn't get around to sowing seed, the garden centres will have a variety of winter vegetable bedding plants available.

The pea patch, which should have finished producing by now, is the best place to plant brussels sprout seedlings. This is because the roots of pea vines are covered with nitrogen nodules that are very useful to your brussels sprouts. When taking away the spent pea vines, make sure to leave the roots in the ground, to be turned under the soil before planting your sprouts. It's also a good idea to add a little lime before planting, as the sprouts prefer a less acid soil.

It is especially important in hot summer weather to prepare your planting bed in advance, before you even lift the little plants. Try to plant in the evening, which will give the seedlings overnight to adjust to the move. Brussels sprouts take up a lot of room at maturity, so plant them at least 75 centimetres (30 inches) apart. You can use the space in between to sow a crop of radishes or lettuce for the August salad bowl.

Surprisingly, you can also sow a late crop of bush or wax beans at this time, if you live in a coastal area. I used to think it was too late to sow these crops, but I have since had great success with it, so I recommend you try it. The beans will be ready by late August to early September.

If you have grown bush beans you have probably fought the battle with black aphids, commonly known as blackfly, with all the available pesticides on the market, and nothing has worked. I have found a method that works, although it may sound a little bizarre.

To begin, collect some leaves that are thickly covered with blackfly. Put them in a kitchen blender that is a little under half-full of water and blend it until it turns to a pulpy, awful-looking, grey-green consistency. Strain the juice, mix it with a little more water, and spray it on the in-   89 fected plants. I guarantee there will not be a blackfly left on them by the next morning.

Finally, there is a good use for that old blender! But if you are going to do this on a regular basis, and you wish to keep your mate, you should probably invest in a blender for bugs.

If your early crops, like lettuce, cauliflower or spring cabbage, haven't quite finished yet, and you want to get your beans going, just soak them three to four hours and sow them in pairs in 10-centimetre (4-inch) pots with regular good garden soil. They'll be ready by the time you have some space in your garden.

The other crop that is ideal for July sowing is carrots. If you have well-drained soil, carrots sown at this time can be left in the ground for harvesting right up until December or later, if the weather remains mild. Of course, any crops you sow should have some initial fertilizer to get them going, such as granular 6-8-6, applied at a handful per square metre (square yard) or an application of well-rotted compost which has been worked into the soil.

Cool Wet Weather

In the June section, there is a discussion of keeping the garden well-watered in the hot summer months and that is what most of us want and expect in the summer. But occasionally we get a summer that provides long periods of cool wet weather, causing problems in the garden and delaying the harvest of food crops. We gardeners always have the weather to hang both our failures and successes on, and that is one of the variables that makes gardening fun. In many ways gardeners are better than politicians when it comes to excuses!

A prolonged spell of cool weather coupled with regular feedings of high-nitrogen fertilizer encourages an over-abundance of leaf growth.

That can lead to serious attacks of fungus diseases, as it cuts down on air circulation. When these conditions are present, don't be afraid to remove some of the bottom leaves of those vegetables that have masses of leaves, even if they are still green and healthy looking. The leaves can be shredded and added to the compost pile, so all is not lost.

Some of the heat-loving vegetables, like zucchini, cucumber and tomatoes, will have a hard time getting going in dull rainy weather. But if your tomatoes can be placed in a protected spot, such as a southwest-facing wall, it will help. If the fruit has started forming, remove some of the leaves that are hiding the fruit, but leave at least one leaf, or a part of it, just below the forming fruit to help with food distribution throughout the plant's system.

Some flowers—zinnias, gazanias and geraniums—simply won't blossom if the weather is too cool and dull. Cut right back on high-nitrogen fertilizer and use more potash, as that's the major element used to form blossoms. Leaf removal isn't usually carried out on flowering plants, but with some plants, like geraniums, removal of some of the leaves may encourage flowering.

Ironically, weeds thrive in this sort of weather, and you can't just pull them and leave them lying around as you can in the sun. They will just reroot and grow again. Try to keep the weeds down, though, as their presence adds to the problem of air circulation.

Finally, slugs seem to love the rain and are a constant menace in the vegetable garden, especially when they chew their way into a head of lettuce, or get up inside the base of a cabbage. These plants will be close to being harvested, so I don't recommend chemical sprays, but you can catch them in homemade slug traps and then dispose of them, as described on page 73.

In your fruit garden, a cold wet start to the season can lead to a rash of fungus diseases later in the year, such as rust on raspberries and pear trellis rust. These can be quite serious problems, which are not easy to deal with.

Pear trellis rust first occurred in B.C. in 1934, probably imported from Europe on infected junipers. The great difficulty with pear trellis rust is that it overwinters on junipers; then in spring, when the leaves come out, spores spread to the pear leaves. There they show up as yel-   91 lowish blotches on the leaf surface and as clusters of rusty-looking, egg-like lumps on the underside of the leaf.

These leaves should be picked off and preferably burned. If the rust really gets a hold, it can completely destroy the fruit. Unfortunately, there is no known cure for this problem, other than digging up and destroying any juniper in the area. This was carried out on a grand scale in the Fraser Valley during the 1970s, in an attempt to eradicate the disease, but it has been coming back again recently.

Houseplants in Summer

It may seem strange to think about houseplants in the middle of the summer, but all kinds of problems can arise at this time of year. For example, the weeping fig (which I believe should never have been introduced as a houseplant) tends to lose its leaves like mad as soon as the weather turns warm. It will do it again in the winter when the heat is turned up high, and the problem is probably connected to the lack of humidity.

You may have had the experience of growing a weeping fig for several years without any problems, only to find one day that the carpet was covered with leaves—even green ones! The only solution I can give is to make sure the plant is kept moist at all times. Mist daily and keep it in good light but away from direct sun. If it is very bald, make a tent from a drycleaning bag or other plastic, like a miniature greenhouse around it. Keep the humidity up until the plant recovers.

Summer feeding is important to all houseplants at this time of year. Feed at least once every two weeks with a weak solution of a liquid fertilizer. I do recommend alternating your plant foods. There can be a real problem of salt building up in the soil, if the same soluble fertilizer is used continuously. Salt build-up can cause leaf drop and scorching.

Some plants, such as Christmas cactus, hibiscus and ornamental flowering azaleas, like to go outdoors in the summer. In fact, if they aren't put outside, they will not flower well during the winter months. The key here is to introduce them to the sun gradually. For more information on putting houseplants outside in the summer, refer to page 84. All winter flowering plants should be fed regularly every two weeks, using liquid fertilizer that has a higher middle and last number, to promote flower buds.

Summer is synonymous with vacation, when you have to figure out what to do with your houseplants while you are away. Of course it is best to find a reliable friend to drop in and water at least once a week, but if that's impossible, try one of the following techniques.

Perhaps the easiest method is to put as many plants as you can in a large clear plastic bag just before you leave, making sure everything is well watered. Completely seal the bag so that it is like a large enclosed terrarium. This is good for up to three weeks as long as the plants are getting good light every day.

A similar but more time-consuming method is to water every plant well and then enclose the pot in individual plastic bags, securing the bag around the base of the stem with a tie. This allows the foliage to be out, while the soil is covered. This can be successful for a couple of weeks.

The last procedure has been used successfully for a period of up to six weeks. Put damp newspapers in the bottom of your bathtub. Then run a hose from the cold tap to the opposite end of the bathtub from the drain and leave the tap dripping. Make sure the drain is unplugged! Water all the plants well and stand them closely together in the bathtub, putting a clear plastic sheet over the top.

This approach relies on a bathroom that has good natural light from a window. If you don't have natural light in the bathroom, you could use a grow-light bulb placed next to the bath. It should be on a timed switch that turns it on for at least twelve hours a day.

Summer Propagation—
Growing Your Own Shrubs

There is a great deal of satisfaction to be derived from growing your own plants. While many of us grow flowers and vegetables from seed, propagation of shrubs from cuttings is often overlooked. If you want to experiment with ways to root new pieces of your favourite shrubs, anytime from the end of July to the last week in August is the ideal time to do it.

I am often asked how to propagate such plants as wisteria or clematis. While they are both propagated readily in the commercial trade by grafting or budding, they are not usually successfully rooted from cuttings at home. However, layering works really well with both these plants.

Wisteria is a vine that has long tassles of purple, fragrant, laburnum-like flowers that bloom in the the spring. At this time of the year, wisteria sends out masses of long new growth.

Choose one or two of the strongest shoots that are near the ground, and look for the area of the shoot where the green becomes more woody and difficult to bend. At that spot, take a little v-shaped nick out of the underside, just below a leaf joint. Then bury the nicked part under about 6 centimetres (2½ inches) of soil, making sure that there is at least 30 centimetres (12 inches) of the growing tip sticking out of the ground. The shoot is still attached to the main stem, of course, but the nick will encourage it to root faster than if it was left whole.

You can then forget about it until next spring, when it should be well rooted and can be severed from the mother plant by pruning.

You can root clematis using the same method, but because the stems are so brittle, it is impossible to nick them. Just bury the stem, keeping it anchored to the ground by placing a small heavy rock over the place it is buried. Many of the true species clematis, like *C. tangeurica* and *C. montana*, will germinate readily from seed.

Another, slightly more complex, way of dealing with shrubs that are more difficult to root, such as camellia or magnolia, is air layering. For this you need some sheets of clear heavy-gauge plastic cut into pieces

94

45 by 30 centimetres (18 by 12 inches), some strong twine or other ties, sphagnum moss (true sphagnum is difficult to find, but it's the one that holds water like a sponge), and a sharp knife.

At this time of year magnolia will have lots of new growth on it, which formed soon after the flowers faded. If you feel the new shoots now, you will find that some of them are tending to get woody and difficult to bend. These are the prime candidates for layering. Choose one that is at least 30 centimetres (12 inches) long, and remove all but the top three or four leaves. Midway down the stem, make an angled cut up behind a leaf joint, being careful to go only halfway into the stem. Bend the stem very carefully to open up the cut a little, then push a small piece of moist moss into the cut to wedge it open. You can use hormone rooting powder on the cut, but if it is forced open wide enough, it shouldn't be necessary.

Place two good handfuls of moist moss around the whole stem, completely covering the cut area. Holding it with one hand, wrap a bandage of the clear plastic all around it, securing it top and bottom with ties to keep the moisture in. If true sphagnum is used it should stay wet for weeks, but if not, you may have to add water to the moss from time to time.

Either in the fall or the spring you should see roots developing in the moss, but don't be tempted to prune the branch before early spring. At that time the plastic can be removed and the new little magnolia planted out.

Shrubs like forsythia, wiegela, and spirea can be rooted from cuttings in a mix of two parts peat to one part sand. There are several ways of rooting the cuttings, but the best method is to root them in a cold frame.

For cuttings, collect semi-hardwood—the new shoots that appeared this spring after flowering and are now getting woody. The pieces you take from the shrubs will most likely have several cuttings on them, so select some of the better-looking shoots and strip them away from the main stem by giving them a sharp downward tug. They will come away with a strip of the old stem attached, which you can trim away horizontally with a sharp razor blade or knife, leaving a minute amount of the old stem on the bottom. This is what is known as a heel cutting.

Make a cutting about 15 centimetres (6 inches) in length, taking a 95 clean horizontal bud directly below the leaf joint. If the tip is very soft, trim it off.

Remove the lower leaves completely and dip the cut end in rooting hormone (number-two strength). Plant the cuttings either in small pots or seed flats, making sure to cover all the leaf joints where the leaves have been removed, as each of those nodes are potential root development areas. Make sure to label your plantings. Water well and keep the cold frame covered for the first few weeks for good humidity, opening it slightly for air circulation and sheltering it from direct sun on hot sunny days.

Another way of rooting cuttings is in old-fashioned clay pots, 15 to 20 centimetres (6 to 8 inches) in size. Make up a propagating mixture of two parts sand or perlite to one part peat. When the cuttings are planted, put the whole pot in a plastic bag and seal it at the top. In some ways this is an easier method, as you can keep an eye on the cuttings. Once they're rooted, they can be potted on.

Keep the cuttings well watered all summer and leave them in the cold frame or pots over winter. Many of the cuttings will have rooted by fall, but it's best not to plant them out before next spring. By then you will have many new shrubs to swap with friends. Don't worry about the cuttings being too small. In a climate like this it won't take more than five years to produce a decent-sized shrub from these seedlings.

Trimming Evergreens

Midsummer is the time for trimming evergreen hedges and pruning evergreen trees. Evergreens such as ornamental cedars and spreading junipers are hardy and widely used throughout B.C. In many cases they are planted close to homes, as tiny and attractive foundation plantings. But following nature's way, they grow, encroaching on lawns, driveways, and pathways. The difficulty then is pruning them while

96

maintaining their natural shape.

Let's start with low-growing spreading junipers. It is possible to prune these plants so that they don't look like a straight hedge. Their sprawling growth habit makes the job easier for you.

You'll need a good sharp pair of pruners and, for older trees, perhaps a pruning saw. Stand back and assess the amount that needs to be reduced and the overall shape. To help get a mental picture, lay some twine or garden hose on the bush as a guideline to follow.

Lifting the longest outer branches will reveal the growth habit to you. You'll notice that each individual branchlet grows out over the base of the one below it, almost the same way that shingles are laid. Choose the level of sideshoot or branch that has its tip closest to the end where your marker is lying. Then cut the main branch well in under the overlapping one, so that the cut is hidden and the little pointed shoot becomes the leader shoot. Do this all around the bush, standing back after every other cut to make sure that you are still on track.

The same method can be followed on prostrate pines and firs, although they are not as commonly grown.

If you want to control the size of pine trees, just reduce the new growth—the soft shoot that is often referred to as candles in gardening books. Do as the traditional Japanese gardeners do—cut each one back to 2 centimetres (¾ inch) or so. It won't hurt them, but will control growth.

Many people plant cedar screening hedges when they first move, to provide privacy. If the hedge is more than two or three years old, it will be surprisingly tall. The most important thing to remember with any cedar or similar hedge is to make sure that it is pruned or topped as soon as it reaches the required height. Many people forget to do it, only to find that ten years have passed and the trees are monstrous. At that stage you'll have to massacre the trees by removing the top half, in order to cut it down to size, thus totally spoiling the natural conical shape. To avoid this problem, trim the hedge annually once it has reached the required height. Not only will the hedge be nicely shaped, it will be bushier as a result.

Summertime is a good time for this pruning work because the annual growth of all evergreens starts in late April or May, depending on 97 where you live, and matures around late July to early August. If the tree is pruned before the new growth is matured, however, it will attempt to put on more growth and will have to be pruned again. Pruning now will also give any exposed growth time to harden up and get acclimatized before winter frosts start. On the coast this isn't critical, perhaps, but don't get too blasé about it. A few years ago, many laurel hedges were frozen when there was a sudden cold spell in November. The hedges that really suffered were those pruned in October.

Speaking of laurel hedges, do take the time to hand prune them. If they are trimmed with hedging or electrical shears, the large leaves get cut in half, which looks ugly, and the leaves eventually turn brown. Don't be afraid to cut into some of the leafless wood, about every other cut or so. This will encourage strong new growth and keep the hedge within bounds.

When trimming an evergreen hedge like yew or privet, line your eye up with a straight wall or something similar on the horizon and cut with that straight line as your guide. Trim the whole hedge lightly the first time, then go back and finish it off, at which time you can level it all out. If you cut too deeply on the first cut, you can't stick pieces back!

Having said that, I must also warn you not to be too tentative with your pruning. It is important to cut back the main body of greenery that was there before new growth started, to keep the overall growth in bounds and to encourage the new growth. If this isn't done each year, when it is finally cut back it will look dreadful for almost a year, as all the dormant wood will be exposed.

The exception to evergreen pruning at this time might be holly. On the coast you could wait until the winter holiday season, when great branches can be cut for decorating your home.

A U G U S T

CHAPTER EIGHT

Preserving
Summer's Colours

With the arrival of August and the height of summer, it's time to think about ways of preserving some of the colour for fall and winter enjoyment. Many flowers, foliage plants, and herbs will dry well and the hot dry days of August are ideal for this task.

Over the years, certain flowers have been established as good for drying. These include statice, helichrysum (strawflowers), and physalis (Chinese lanterns). But there are many others that will dry well and keep their colour if dried properly. Above all, they must be dried quickly, as speed is the key to drying.

Outdoor air drying is the best, and can be done quite successfully on a clothesline. The tools are simple: some good sharp pruners, strong garden twine, and a container into which you can strip the leaves.

Cut the flowers in the late morning when they are nice and dry, and strip off all the foliage, even though it sounds drastic. If you leave it on, it will become quite unsightly, and when dry it will crumble and make a mess.

Make the bunches small, about ten stems, keeping the same   99 varieties or species together. Tie them together securely and hang them up with the flower heads hanging down. This will give them strong, straight, stiff stems. Take the flowers in each night and put them out again in the morning.

The flowers should be gathered before they have been pollinated. For example, if strawflowers aren't gathered before the open middle is showing, the seeds will form and the whole flower will shatter when it dries. Pick larkspur, an old-fashioned annual delphinium, just when the first six or so blossoms have opened on the spike and the top is still nicely in bud.

Depending on the weather, flowers can take up to a week to dry, at which time they can be hung in the basement or other storage area. Cover them with light plastic or paper bags to keep the dust off until you're ready to use them. Paper is better than plastic, simply because if there is any small amount of moisture left in them, plastic will cause rotting.

If you like to make your own cards, some pretty effects can be achieved using dried and pressed flowers. The flowers can be dried in a proper flower press, or simply placed between the pages of an old phone book, or other heavy book. To maintain their lovely shapes, select single flower heads and carefully place them on the paper, placing another sheet across the top before pressing.

Foliage can be preserved to decorate your house over the winter, using the glycerine method. Many leaves can be preserved, so be sure to experiment, but salal, beech, and laurel leaves all work well. You'll need glycerine, which can be purchased from a drugstore, and a large-mouthed jar, such as a commercial pickle jar. Mix one part glycerine to two parts water in the jar.

Cut short, useable branches of the selected type, and before putting the stems in the glyerine mixture, bash them a little to help take up the water faster. You will notice that the mixture is absorbed quickly and the next day it will need topping up with water (do not add more glycerine). In a week or so, the foliage will have turned a dark olive to brownish colour. When the leaves are all evenly coloured and some drops of excess glycerine show up on the leaf surface, take the branches out of the mixture, bundle them up and hang them upside-down.

They'll dry nicely and may be successfully used for several years.

When it comes to herbs, some people have mastered the knack of drying them really quickly in a toaster or microwave oven, but that needs careful practice. I still like to do mine in the sun.

Herbs can be dried by tying them up in bunches, like the flowers, but a better method is to make a small hammock out of a piece of sheer material such as muslin. Place the herbs inside and hang it on the clothesline in full sun. Throughout the day, shake the material from time to time, to redistribute the plants and even out the drying process. When they're completely dry (a couple of days), crumble the dried leaves carefully into a paper bag and then put them into an airtight container, for use in the kitchen during the dull days of winter.

Last but not least, you probably have the ingredients for a sweet-smelling potpourri right in your garden. The petals of fragrant varieties of rose, carnations, honeysuckle and lavendar all work well. Gather the petals in midmorning and dry them in shallow containers in a dark, dry place. Once dry, mix 625 millilitres (2½ cups) dried petals with 125 millilitres (½ cup) orris root powder, 15 millilitres (1 tablespoon) ground cinnamon, 7 millilitres (½ tablespoon) ground nutmeg and twelve whole cloves. Mix well, place in a large jar, and stir through 15 millilitres (1 tablespoon) of orris root powder mixed with 5 millilitres (1 teaspoon) rose oil. Cover and stir occasionally over the next month, when it will be ready to use.

These are just a few ways of preserving the colours, smells and tastes of summer—enough to whet your interest. You'll find quite a lot of literature on the subject at your library or bookstore and I would encourage you to try some of the ideas. Making a summer garden last all winter is well worth it.

Flowers from Cuttings and Seeds

At the height of the summer season, it may seem a little odd to be looking ahead to next year's show. But if you're planning on saving some seed, or perhaps taking cuttings of your favourite geraniums, think about doing it now. It may seem slightly early, as traditionally everyone waits until the fall, but if you are like me, cuttings taken in the fall have a 50 percent or higher failure rate. That high rate is because plants have already started to slow to their winter growing pace by the fall, and it is more difficult to maintain warmer temperatures, no matter where you are rooting the cuttings.

You should be aware that it isn't always possible to save seed of an annual you like and have it come true to the same type and colour the next year. This is because it has likely been cross-pollinated with pollen from other gardens. However, certain annuals lend themselves well to seed collecting, and they are worth a place in your garden every year—candytuft, bachelor's buttons, and shirley poppies are in this category.

For the plants you want to propagate, now is the time to stop picking off deadheads; instead let them form into seed pods. After about a week, on a hot sunny day when the morning dew has dried, collect the seed heads into brown paper bags, one for each variety, and label them with a permanent marker as you collect. Leave the bags in the sun to dry for the remainder of the day, making sure that they are well anchored so they don't blow away, and take them indoors at night. Repeat this procedure for about a week, at which time the pods should open and release the seed into the bag. Now the seed can be transferred into small envelopes, labelled and sealed, and popped into an airtight container. The best storage place is the crisper drawer of your fridge, but if that's not possible, keep them in a room that maintains a constant cool temperature. Heat destroys the viability of seeds quite rapidly.

The same sort of process will apply to seeds from your vegetable garden, but it will occur later, perhaps early October for such crops as pole beans, broad beans, or even onions if you let them go to seed.

Now to the cuttings. Before going further, I should clarify that the annual plants most of us call geraniums are not geraniums at all, they are zonal pelargoniums. For some reason, they have been misnamed for years. At this time of year, what we know as geraniums have many strong shoots, most of which will have flowers on them. Without totally ruining your colourful plants, carefully choose a couple of strong shoots from each plant, cutting them at least 15 centimetres (6 inches) long. Put the cuttings straight into a plastic bag until you are ready to work with them.

Any book on propagation will tell you to collect shoots for cuttings that do not have flowers on them, which at this time of year is almost impossible. There is a reason for this suggestion, however: if the cutting is in flower or bud, it will expend its energy flowering and seeding. To prevent that, remove the flowers and buds from the cuttings you choose.

To begin, cut strong-looking shoots at least 15 centimetres (6 inches) long, and don't restrict yourself to geraniums; choose from marguerite daisies, fibrous-rooted begonias and even gazanias.

When they are all collected, prepare them with a sharp paring knife. Cut them between 12 and 15 centimetres (4 to 6 inches) long, making a clean horizontal cut directly below a leaf joint. Remove any blossoms or flower buds and all the leaves from the bottom half, leaving three or four good ones near the top. Fuchsia cuttings will tend to have very soft tops that will wilt if left on, so pinch the top out to just above the strongest leaves.

Thoroughly mix and moisten the rooting medium before putting it in the pots. Dip the cut ends of all the cuttings into a rooting hormone, using number one strength for softwood cuttings. Push them into the mix, making sure that half of the cutting is buried. Each of the leaf joints is a potential root-producing area.

Place them five to a 15-centimetre (6-inch) pot. If you have quite a few cuttings it might be easier to root them in a seed flat, rather than flower pots. Interestingly, cuttings rooted in old-fashioned clay pots root faster than those in plastic. The reason seems to be plenty of air getting to the mix.

If you're using individual pots, cover them with clear plastic bags, like   103 a mini-greenhouse. It may be sealed for all cuttings except geraniums and pelargoniums, which will rot before they root if it is too humid. Place them on a window ledge out of full sunlight. If you're using a cold frame or greenhouse, watch that the sun doesn't shine directly on them from mid-morning to mid-afternoon. At these times, protect them from direct sun by covering them with newspaper. For all plantings the mix must be kept moist.

After about two weeks the cuttings should be nicely rooted, at which time you can pot them on into individual pots about the size of styrofoam coffee cups. (In fact, these work really well with a few holes poked in the bottom.) At this stage you should use good sterilized potting mix, as the new plants will be living in it until early next spring.

If you don't have greenhouse space, remember to root only as many plants as your windowsill can hold for the winter. It is very easy to get carried away and not have room for you and your family in the house. But I do urge you to try softwood cuttings at this time of the year; all of them will root well.

Late Summer Sun and Summer Maintenance

The welcome sun of late summer helps bring vegetables such as corn and tomatoes to a perfect ripeness. If you haven't done so, now is the time to pinch out the tops of your tomato plants; it will stop them from growing any more greenery and divert the plant's energy to fruit development and ripening.

If it's your first year gardening in B.C., you may be horrified at how quickly everything turns brown in dry weather. Much of the province's soil is porous, letting water drain away quickly in wet times. But don't be alarmed; the green will all come back as soon as the fall rains come.

Once there is a return to the normal moist weather pattern, it is a good idea to feed the lawn with a high phosphate fertilizer to get some good root action going again. In a really dry spell, the leaves of trees can turn brown and drop prematurely, but here again, even if you can't water them, they will survive until the rains come. But do make sure to water all those trees and shrubs that were newly planted this year, as they haven't had a chance to develop a really good root system yet.

This is the time when fertilizing or feeding flowers and vegetables is most important. You should be using something like granular 6-8-6 on your garden once a month during June, July, and August. Spread it at about a handful per square metre (square yard) just before rain, or, in a dry spell, just before watering. If it isn't watered down, some of the fertilizer might get caught in the leaves and burn the plants.

Tomatoes in the garden could use some extra phosphate and potash around now. The phosphate will increase the root system and the potash will boost the fruit. I would suggest a half a handful per plant of a combination of superphosphate and sulphate of potash mixed together. Container tomatoes can be fed with 6-8-6 or 0-15-14, the latter sold under the trade name of Sturdy.

It is most important in dry weather to keep tomatoes watered. They should never dry out at the root. If they do, you will get blossom end rot, which shows up when the fruit is ripe. The blossom end cells of the tomato dry out, and when you pick a tomato, you'll find that it is black and hard on the bottom.

With leaf crops like cabbage, brussels sprouts, and celery, sprinkle on a quarter handful of ammonium sulphate or urea per square metre (square yard). They are high nitrogen and therefore good for leaf and stem development. But they burn, so water it in right away.

Pole and bush beans should be producing fast and furiously at this point. Try to keep them picked every day so that they continue to produce well into September. In some years there is a problem with blossoms dropping off scarlet runners and other pole beans. This can occur when the nights are too cool. Red-flowered varieties need temperatures of 20 to 25°C (68 to 77°F) to set properly, and white and pink forms will tolerate 15°C (59°F). But when the season is hot and dry, blossom drop is more likely caused by insufficient water or too much nitrogen in the soil. If that is a problem, here is a tip to tuck away for next year, when you're preparing your bean trench.

Select the site in the fall and dig out about 60 centimetres (2 feet) of soil. Over the winter, gradually fill in the trench with household waste, such as vegetable peelings and fruit rinds. My mentor in the UK, Mrs. Frances Perry, also shredded up newspapers and thoroughly wet them down before burying them in the bottom of her bean trench. Gradually fill the trench over the winter so that by spring the trench will be full of well-rotted, moisture-retaining compost.

SEPTEMBER

CHAPTER NINE

Making Summer Last

The summer flowers always seem to hit their peak in early September. This is the time when gardeners can really enjoy the fruits of their labours. By following a few practices you can extend the season and keep all that colour until the first frost, or at least mid-October.

The key to keeping a good annual display going at this time of year is to make sure that deadheads are picked off regularly. An annual's prime objective is to flower and make seed for the following year, so if the seed heads are picked off just before maturity, the plant will automatically go about making new flower buds. While it isn't possible to deadhead all annuals—nemesia is a good example—picking the blossoms of flowers such as sweet peas will result in many more blooms.

Once nemesia, linaria and Virginia stock have bloomed, they are really finished, and that is one reason they should always be planted among other flowers. Good choices are fibrous rooted begonias and geraniums, which will take over quite nicely this far along in the summer. The begonias actually do better with the onset of cooler nights, and their colours even seem to improve with the late summer sun.

Fuchsias also seem to enjoy the cooler nights. Fuchsias set lots of seed, particularly if the hummingbirds are constant visitors (they pollinate the flowers when they extract the nectar). The seeds look like small, soft, fleshy plums. Try to keep them picked off as they appear, although if they are left on the fuchsia won't stop flowering completely.

Delphiniums, poppies, and lupins will have finished flowering long ago, and should be cut back by now (not all the way to the ground, but into the green leafy part). If you feed them, you may get a second flowering in the fall, particularly with the delphiniums. Generally speaking, all feeding should cease at this time, with the exception of hanging baskets and containers. Even there, it should be a weak feeding only once a week.

If you sowed wallflowers, Canterbury bells, or primroses last June, they'll be coming along nicely now. For the first two, pinch back their tops so that they form bushy plants and feed them with granular 6-8-6 to build up their root system for transplanting at the end of September or mid-October.

In the vegetable garden, the bean plants will just keep producing as long as you pick the beans off. However, it's always nice to leave a few on for seed, and if your bushes are producing more than you can eat, you might want to dry some for soup in the winter.

Tomatoes need a hot growing season and at this time of the year there are often many unripe tomatoes on the plants. The key is to leave the fruit on the plant as long as possible. If the weather is still sunny, leave the plants in the ground until just before frost, then cut the whole plant at the ground or pull it up by the roots. Remove all the leaves and flowers and hang the vines with the green tomatoes on them in a protected shed or garage to let them ripen on the vine. It doesn't have to be light, as tomatoes will ripen even in the dark. Those that are already showing colour can be picked to finish the ripening process in your kitchen.

If you planned your garden to include an area for a winter garden, your leeks and parsnips should be coming along well. If they aren't looking too healthy, I am all in favour of using a liquid seaweed or fish fertilizer, which are both fairly high in nitrogen, to give them a boost right now, as long as the weather is still warm.

For those who live on the coast, if you have some room, why not experiment with some of the Chinese green vegetables, such as bok choy. It enjoys a cooler growing season, and if there is a long fall season, it will produce greens for stir-fried vegetables. Even a late sowing of spinach would be worth a try. It is a gamble, but would be well worth the effort for that fresh spinach salad harvested from your own garden in mid-October. One of the great thrills of gardening in coastal B.C. is the fact that severe winter weather sometimes never comes and growing can go on well into fall and even winter.

Garden Evaluation

Right now, when the flower garden is at its peak, and the vegetables are almost ready to harvest, is the time to look at your garden as a whole and record the good and bad points. For example, in my own garden I got quite a bit of afternoon shade from some very nice copper beech trees, and one September I made a sketch and note of which branches I intended to prune out, once the leaves had dropped in late fall.

However, even with the branches gone, I still needed to choose the annuals for that area more carefully, leaning more towards the shade-lovers like begonias, fuchsias and monkey flower (mimulus). One year I used all snapdragons and poor-man's orchid, and they all fell over, particularly after watering. I had to support each snapdragon with an individual cane; not only was it time-consuming, but they looked very unnatural.

The point is that now is the time to look at your garden, to see what worked and what didn't, and make notes for next year. Part of the fun of gardening is that it is a constant learning process, even when you've been doing it for many years.

In a vegetable garden, you should never plant the same crop in the same space year after year. It robs the soil of the same food elements, resulting in poorer crops. If you haven't already done so, sketch your vegetable area, so that next year you can change your planting pattern.

The right colour combinations in the flower garden can be very striking. Those of you who like to read about, or visit, other gardens when you go overseas will know about 'Sissinghurst', the famous garden of Vita Sackville-West in Kent, England. She had an incredible talent for planting the right colours together, and she achieved it by cutting a flower and then holding it against a plant that she thought it might go well with. If it worked, those flowers were planted together next season. The result is beautifully pleasing to the eye.

You can achieve your own beautiful effects in a home garden, or even a balcony or patio, so get out there and make notes to yourself right now, while everything is still in place. You can then spend the dark days of fall and winter planning a spectacular show or productive vegetable garden for next year.

Now is also a good time to be thinking of how to enrich your soil with compost, with all that natural potential compost lying around in the form of leaves. You can never overdo adding organic material to the soil, and as the garden begins to fade during the next few weeks, it's a good idea to start up a temporary compost right in the garden.

All you need is some chicken wire and four sturdy stakes just over a metre (3 feet) in length. Choose a site and place the stakes in each corner of a square metre (3-foot-square) area. Attach the wire to three sides, making the open side sheltered from prevailing winds. That way your compost material, such as leaves, won't blow all over the garden.

As you rake the leaves, pull up plants, remove the lower leaves from plants or deadhead the dahlias, throw it all on the heap. Every time you have a 15-centimetre (6-inch) layer of garden waste, sprinkle on some ammonium sulphate. Keep building, and by spring it will be humus. For more ideas on composting, see page 128.

September Tidy-up

E ven though it's September, don't feel that you have to put the garden to bed already. But if you're itching to get at some garden chores, there are a few tidying-up things that can be tackled now.

If you have any of those old-fashioned rambler roses that only bloom once early in the season, and then produce nothing but long, rather untidy shoots from the base, you can cut out the old wood now. Cut it as close to the ground as possible, then tie in the new shoots, which are the basis of all next summer's flowers, in a fan design, or whatever suits the space it is in. Ramblers are the only roses that should be pruned now; all others should be left until early spring.

The only fruiting plants that can be safely pruned at this time are the raspberries, blackberries, tayberries and the like. Cut out all the vines that have borne fruit this season and tie in the new ones, much like the rambler roses. If you live in the Interior, wait until January or February for this job.

Perennials that are looking a little untidy in the flower border can be trimmed back as well. Do it with care—just to the base of the flower stem. I know it is tempting to cut them all the way down, but if you do you will destroy all of nature's winter blanket.

Some of the plants in your garden, such as eucalyptus and early-blooming camellias, may be only borderline hardy. While it's still too early to cover them for the winter, you may want to consider building chicken-wire fences around them at this time. Push four sturdy stakes into the ground at the edges of the plant's branches, and run some chicken wire around them, securing it to the posts. Later in the month, gradually fill in the cage loosely with dry leaves, which will protect the plant from a severe frost.

Quite a few people in southern coastal areas have edible figs in their garden. In a good sunny year, they can produce a lot of fruit, but in order to make them ripen, you'll have to build a temporary greenhouse shelter out around the tree, using plastic sheeting. A Greek friend now living in Vancouver has his figs planted along a west-facing wall and trained loosely on wires. At the top of the wall he has permanent brack- 111 ets that stick out 60 centimetres (2 feet). At this time of the year he has clear heavy-gauge plastic sheeting on rollers that are attached to the top and can be raised and lowered according to the weather. When it gets cool and wet later in the fall, he leaves them on permanently until all the fruit has ripened. All this trouble is well worth it, believe me, because there is nothing like a fresh fig straight from the tree.

If you have a greenhouse, September is a good time to clean it out and make it ready for winter storage of tender plants. Choose a sunny day, so that any plants you already have in the greenhouse won't be damaged by being outside for the day. After clearing the greenhouse, hose down the entire inside surfaces and scrub any dirty benches or glass with a good household disinfectant. This will help eliminate fungus and other diseases that may be lurking there. Then give the whole place another hosing down and allow the late summer sun to dry it all out before putting the plants back inside.

Follow the same procedure if you have a cold frame. For both structures, make sure you catch all the crevices and corners where insects could lay their eggs. Many insects are smarter than you might think and fall is the time when they re-establish themselves in a warm greenhouse—it is almost as good as going to Hawaii for the winter. So get them out now, to cut down on problems next spring.

Cold Frames and Greenhouses

I suppose that all gardeners, at one time or another, wish for a greenhouse. The need is more obvious in the spring, when you want to grow your own bedding plants and so on, but the fall is a good time to consider building one too. Provided the greenhouse is in the right location, with good air circulation, you will be able to successfully overwinter many of the plants blooming right now in your garden, such as marguerites, fuchsias, and pelargoniums, particularly in the coastal areas.

The most useful and economic way to start off with a greenhouse is with a cool one. That means having some kind of minimal heating for the coldest winter months. A good temperature to aim for is 8°C (48°F). A cold greenhouse, exactly as it's name implies, has no heat. During sunny weather it will warm up and it will be good for starting early crops in the spring, but it won't be useful for overwintering tender plants like fuchsias.

Greenhouses come in all sizes, and once you get hooked on greenhouse growing, no matter what size you have, it won't be large enough. But my advice is to start off with a 3- by 9-metre (10- by 30-foot) base. It should have a bench and shelving on one side and be open on the other. The open side could have removable shelving that would be useful for winter storage or spring bedding plant production, but could be removed later to give room to grow tomatoes or cucumbers.

A greenhouse should be sited in the sunniest spot in your garden, which will cut down on heating costs in the winter and give your plants a good start in the early spring. An alternative to the freestanding greenhouse is to build a conservatory-type greenhouse against a south-facing wall of your home. It will save a lot on heating.

There has been much discussion on the relative merits of having a greenhouse run north-south or east-west. I tend to favour north-south, as that way you get the full advantage of early morning and late afternoon sun. The problem of too much sun in the spring and summer months can be dealt with by shading.

If there is a choice of building a greenhouse on a soil base or a concrete base, by all means go for the latter. It will be easier to keep clean, and greenhouse hygiene is a very important point.

If possible, get electricity to the greenhouse. It is the easiest, cleanest way to heat and it is nice to have light, not only for your convenience in the dark days of winter, but also for boosting early spring growth when natural sunlight is often missing. Another convenience, and a good investment, is an automatic vent opener.

However, these are just a few basic pointers, and you will need to read up on the subject if you're seriously considering constructing a greenhouse. There are some good greenhouse books available now. One of my favourites is *How to Build and Use Greenhouses*, which is one of the excellent Ortho books. It is well illustrated and easy to follow.

Whether you construct your own greenhouse or decide to have one built depends on your skill at construction. There is a greenhouse called "Goodlife," which is imported from the UK and available through your local garden centre. B.C. Greenhouse Builders, located in Burnaby, is a local company. Even if you don't purchase a greenhouse from them, their shop carries all the latest equipment you have ever dreamed of for running a successful home greenhouse.

If you can't afford the space or money for a greenhouse, a well-constructed cold frame can be invaluable. It has the advantage of being portable, so you can move it to the warmest spot in your garden, or into the shade in the hot months. A description of how to build a cold frame is on page 55.

Don't underestimate the usefulness of a cold frame. With the protection of a south- or west-facing wall it can be used for growing quick late crops like spinach, winter lettuce or even a late crop of radishes. You can grow very successful herb gardens in it, and they can be used, with some extra protection during severe winter cold spells, for overwintering fuchsias and pelargoniums.

Indoor Gardens

Even though summer is by no means over, the Labour Day weekend always triggers thoughts of the coming winter. Indoor gardening can truly brighten up the grey days of fall and winter, so this is a good time to think about creating a dish garden.

A dish garden is really a miniature living landscape. First you need a suitable container, so look through your attic or junk closet. A big old-fashioned soup tureen or a chamber pot are both perfect. There are also some nice modern-looking containers available, or good old-fashioned terra cotta bowls about 35 centimetres (14 inches) across and 15 centimetres (6 inches) deep.

The traditional bowl will usually have a drainage hole in the bottom, which protects against overwatering. With containers that have no drainage, you must be very careful, as overwatering can cause instant bogs and sure death. With careful planning from the start this problem can be overcome. Find an old piece of garden hose and cut it in a short length just shy of the depth of the container. When filling your dish, place the piece of hose on its end in the deepest part of the dish, and fill in and plant all around it so that it is completely hidden from view. Later, when your dish garden looks dry, dip a homemade dipstick into the inside of the hose. If it shows moisture, then you don't need to water, but if it's dry, add a measured amount of water.

All dish gardens should have a 5-centimetre (2-inch) layer of drainage material in the bottom (styrofoam cups or plastic containers broken into pieces). Purchase some good indoor potting soil, or make your own (page 42). If your soil mix has no fertilizer added, mix in 15 millilitres (1 tablespoon) of an all-purpose granular fertilizer per pailful of soil mix.

If you haven't rooted some houseplants of your own, purchase plants in 10-centimetre (4-inch) pots, selecting those with complementary colours. For example, you might choose a 'Silver Queen' pothos with a white variegation, add a silver-hued peperomia, and for a little colour a pink African violet. For a gold effect, try a spider plant, break fern and golden sweatmoss.

Water the plants at least a few hours before replanting. Place them "pot thick"—with their root areas touching—the taller ones in the centre and the shorter ones to the outside. Fill in gently but firmly with your moistened potting mix, until the container is filled within a few centimetres (1 inch) of the rim. Then mist thoroughly to wash the soil off the leaves and moisten them well.

Your garden should be placed near a south-facing window where it   115 will get good light but not direct sun, until October. At that time, the plants will start to appreciate all light. Don't forget to turn the pot at least monthly for even growth.

Bulbs for Spring

By late September all those super Dutch bulbs are in the garden centres, and each year I think the selection gets better. The earlier you purchase them, the better the selection will be, but there is plenty of time to get the bulbs into the ground—right up until the end of November on the south coast. Newly purchased bulbs can be stored in a cool, dry place that has an even temperature.

Perhaps the most important thing to remember—no matter how few or many bulbs you can afford—is to plant them in clumps of five or more. There is nothing worse than ten tulip bulbs spaced at 30-centimetre (12-inch) intervals in a single row down the side of the driveway. They'll hardly be noticed. But clumps will catch the eye and draw many admiring glances.

When choosing bulbs, keep in mind that daffodil and narcissi are really the best bulbs for our soil and climate. They have staying power, coming up year after year with little help. (Naturally, they enjoy a little plant food now and again.) Tulips are not as good for lasting unless you have just the right spot and soil conditions. However, if you are selecting for long-term plantings, the 'Darwin' types are said to be the best. In any case, the bold and brilliant show of tulips is a must for the spring garden.

Hyacinths, with their intoxicating scent, should be included in any spring garden as well. They are also a bit fussy about soil conditions. There are many varieties of bulbs to choose from, but first you should know a little about the best soil type and location for planting.

116   All bulbs like well-drained soil, but they also require a certain level of

organic material in the soil for moisture retention. (All the bulb-producing areas of Holland have that wonderful reclaimed soil which is rich with humus.) Probably the worst location for bulbs is in a low area of the garden where puddles form during our fall and winter rains.

Sun is also an important factor. Bulbs may bloom in the shade the first season, but they won't thereafter.

When you're ready to plant, assess your soil. If you're planting in an already established flower border, dig your holes about 25 centimetres (10 inches) deep and 30 to 45 centimetres (12 to 18 inches) in diameter. You can plant your bulbs as close as 5 centimetres (2 inches) apart, which will make for an eye-catching display next year. For the best effect, don't mix the bulbs all together in one hole, but keep varieties and types together in one location.

Work about 15 millilitres (a tablespoon) of powdered bone-meal into the bottom of the hole. set your tulips or daffodils in place, approximately 4 centimetres (1½ inches) apart, and cover them in. They should be planted at a depth just a little deeper than a trowel blade's depth (or for large bulbs, a trowel and a half) so that they won't be disturbed when it's time to plant out the bedding plants next year.

Smaller bulbs like crocus, scilla, and snowdrops can't be planted as deeply, which means that if they are in a mixed border, they'll have to be lifted next spring to make way for annuals. I would strongly recommend using these smaller bulbs under deciduous shrubs like forsythia or flowering quince, where they can be left undisturbed for years. Better yet, naturalize them in a lawn area, especially at the base of a tree.

If you have a problem with voles eating your bulbs, when you've dug your hole, line it with a medium- to small-meshed chicken wire. If pheasants are a problem, place some mesh on top of the bulbs as well.

Bulbs for patio containers and pots are best grown on in small pots with good drainage holes. Hyacinths should be planted in individual 10-centimetre (4-inch) pots which can be buried in the garden for the worst of the winter months. Daffodils and narcissi can be planted two layers deep in 15 by 17-centimetre (6- by 7-inch) plastic nursery pots. Bury all these pots in a 30-centimetre (12-inch) trench, in an area of your garden that is protected from winter flooding and cold winds. If you can't bury them, build a chicken wire cage around the pots and   117 cover them with leaves or straw. This will let the rain in while protecting against freezing and thawing, which will quickly cause the bulbs to rot.

By using the pot method, you can lift the pots in February and either tap the bulbs out and plant them in patio containers, or leave them in the pots and relocate them to where you want them, just barely burying them. An attractive covering for pots of hyacinths is moss. The light green really suggests spring.

A couple suggestions for patio planters are anemone and ranunculus. Anemone bulbs look rather like giant, slightly oval, dried raisins. They should be planted on their sides as it's absolutely impossible to tell top from bottom. At least, planted on their sides, they have the choice of growing up. Ranunculus look like miniature dahlia tubers and should be planted with the claw down. The secret of success is to soak them for two hours before planting.

One final thought—you must plant a clump of crocus bulbs in your garden where they can be seen from a kitchen or livingroom window. Some of the early crocus species, such as *C. chrysanthus,* will bloom as early as February, and there is nothing more spirit-lifting than the first crocus blossoms of the season. Especially when they are wide open in that early warm sunshine.

Winter Planters

B elieve it or not, by mid-September it's time to start organizing the winter planting, and the garden centres all have a good selection of winter pansies and other bedding plants.

For some years the UBC Botanical Garden has had some excellent hanging baskets, using many unusual plants not usually associated with this type of planting. A few years ago, they made up some hanging baskets for winter, and although it may sound a little far-fetched, for mild coastal areas it is a wonderful idea. It can even work in a slightly colder environment, where a glassed-in unheated porch can be brightened up all winter long with these baskets.

If you already have hanging summer baskets that you're just putting to bed, you can use the same baskets. Scoop out the old soil, leaving the moss in. (It should still be fine if the baskets have been well fed and watered.) Use fresh soil mix, in the proportions recommended for hanging baskets (see page 53). Fertilizer is not as important for the winter months, but if you want to add something, 30 millilitres (2 tablespoons) of powdered bone-meal can be added to each basket before planting.

Winter heathers, *Erica carnea*, have always been some of my favourite plants, and there are some good specimens available. They range in colour from white through pink to deep magenta and will bloom for three months of the winter. Winter pansies are also a good choice for planters. (Despite some of my earlier opinions on winter pansies, they have proved themselves over the last few years.)

To add to these two flowering plants, there are all kinds of interesting hardy foliage plants to choose from. Some of these are *Hypericum calicynum*, 'Rose of Sharon', periwinkle, and many small conifers. Winter hanging baskets are a one-season planting, and any permanent plants you use, such as the heathers, can be moved to a more permanent home in a garden next spring.

The secret to all hanging baskets is to plant them "pot thick" from the outset—so that all the root balls of the plants are touching. The result is quite stunning and an instant show. Hang the basket next to a doorway, where it will be slightly warmer, and preferably in a location that will catch all the available sun.

A patio planter or half-barrel could also be utilized to provide colour and beauty during the winter. Ornamental kale is an attractive plant with purple or white variegated leaves. Try combining about three purple kale in the centre of a planter, and surround them with a mixture of pink winter heather alternating with blue pansies. Another striking colour combination is white kale with white winter heather and yellow winter pansies.

Experiment with these or your own favourite colour combinations. The result will be eye-catching indeed. 119

OCTOBER

CHAPTER TEN

Flowers for Christmas

Having just dealt with spring bulbs for your garden, let's go on to bulbs that have been specially prepared for forcing. Forcing is really a terrible word for this technique, and I have a dear friend who insists that one coerces bulbs into bloom! No matter what you call it, this is the time to plant bulbs like hyacinths, narcissi and tulips in pots to bloom indoors during the holiday season.

When you are selecting bulbs at your garden centre, you will see certain boxes marked "suitable for forcing." It means that they have been put through a refrigeration period that makes them feel like they have been through winter already. When you plant them they'll start to grow right away and will bloom around Christmas time. If you plant up several consecutive pots, you can have blossoms right through January.

My first experience of forcing bulbs to bloom was when I was in school. For the experiment we used jars shaped a little like an hourglass, wider on the bottom than the top. They had an opening on the top just large enough to hold a single hyacinth bulb.

The bottom was filled with water to within 2 centimetres (¾ inch) of the base of the bulb. Before putting the bulb in place, a piece of charcoal was added to the water to keep it sweet. The jars were then placed in a cold dark cupboard (in England, I hasten to add, this is not too difficult to find). The ideal temperature is 5°C (41°F). We checked them daily to top up the water and measured the roots weekly. After ten weeks in this cold dark place, the roots had fully developed to fill the jar and the top was well underway, about 7 centimetres (3 inches) in height. For the next two weeks, the jars were stood on the classroom window ledge, where the temperature was around 12°C (54°F). This allowed the leaves and flower spikes to develop, so that when we took them home to our parents at the Christmas break, the flowers were ready to bloom.

This method can be used for forcing any bulbs that have been specially prepared, which include hyacinths, narcissi, double early tulips and some of the crocuses. Hyacinths can be grown in water along with paperwhite narcissi, if you have a cold, dark place to store them, such as an unheated garden shed or garage. But I think it is better to grow forcing bulbs in a potting mix, as they can be buried in a trench in the garden.

Hyacinths and crocus can be grown in individual 10-centimetre (4-inch) pots, but I would suggest 15-centimetre (6-inch) pots for the narcissi and early double tulips. When planting tulips, check that the flat side of the bulb is facing the centre of the pot, as tulips send out their flowers from the base of the bulb up the flat side. All the bulbs should be buried beneath the surface of the soil, with the exception of the hyacinths, who prefer to have their necks just poking out of the soil. Most important, label each pot with a permanent marker pen as it is planted up.

A few varieties of hyacinth recommended for forcing are 'Pink Pearl', 'Delft Blue' and 'Carnegie', which is pure white. For double early tulips try the lovely pink 'Peach Blossom', 'Orange Nassau' and 'Mr. van der Hoef', which is an exquisite golden yellow. Amongst the narcissi, 'Paperwhites' and 'Soleil d'Or' are both superbly scented.

Narcissi and tulips can both be layered to give a fuller effect. Place a layer of soil in the bottom of the pot, approximately 5 centimetres (2 inches) deep, then place in three bulbs and cover them so that their tops   121 just show. In the spaces between the bulbs, place in three more, and finally, one in the middle, covering them all with soil to within a few centimetres (1 inch) of the pot's rim. The bulbs on the bottom aren't affected by being planted deeper, and they'll all come up together to give a terrific show.

Once all the pots are planted, dig a trench in a well-drained area of your garden about 45 centimetres (18 inches) deep. If it seems that water will gather in the trench, put a layer of sand in the bottom. Place the pots into the trench and refill it.

Once buried, make a note to yourself on the calendar in red pen when the bulbs should be lifted. The first ones should not be before December 11, which will just have them blooming by Christmas. They don't have to be lifted then, however, and they will be even more appreciated during the dull, wintry days of January. If you leave some pots in the ground until around Christmas, you'll have a burst of January colour.

When the pots are first dug and brought into the house in December, it's important for them to be kept at cooler than average room temperature, no warmer than 12 to 14°C (54 to 58°F) for a couple of weeks. This allows the leaves and buds to develop.

Many people keep their amaryllis over from year to year, and if yours have been drying and baking in the summer sunshine (page 12), now is the time to shake them out of their pots, getting rid of all the old soil and repotting them into some fresh potting mix. Amaryllis started at the beginning of October will bloom during the dull days of November. If you want them for Christmas, hold off starting them for another month.

Pot size for repotting will depend on the size of your bulb, but the pot should be at least twice the diameter of the bulb. I have a double bulb that usually gets potted into a 17-centimetre (7-inch) pot. You have a choice of pots, but I think that red or rusty-coloured amaryllis look at home in old-fashioned terra cotta pots. If using clay, don't forget to soak them for at least half an hour before planting.

Amaryllis bulbs should only be two-thirds buried, so that the neck sits up above the soil level. Place the pot on a north- or east-facing window ledge to start off with, for perhaps two weeks, then move it to a south-facing window. Once it has started to grow, feed it every other week with a low-nitrogen liquid fertilizer.

One other flower you should be working on now for Christmas is that poinsettia you managed to keep over from last year. The poinsettia is native to the more tropical parts of the world, where the nights begin to last about twelve hours at this time of the year. This is what triggers the poinsettia to flower and so you must simulate these long nights.

From this time on it needs at least fourteen hours of complete darkness every night and good light for the remaining hours. A cool closet or a large box with a black garbage bag cover will work, but whatever you do, don't leave it in the dark for more than twenty-four hours!

In all honesty, trying to get a poinsettia to bloom again is very difficult, but if you like a challenge, then it's for you.

Putting the Garden to Bed

Towards the end of October, it's time to get serious about putting the garden to bed. Any time now the first frost can come, although on the coast it's really a waiting and guessing game, as some winters are so mild.

Dahlias, tuberous begonias, gladioli, and other summer bulbs are best left in the ground until the frost blackens their tops. Once this has happened, lift them immediately, removing as much excess soil as possible. If the ground is very wet they may need washing. Remove the dead tops, leaving about 15 centimetres (6 inches) of stem. Begonias will lose their entire top after frost.

If the dahlia tubers are massed and you want to divide them, now is the time to do it, while they are green. Use a sharp knife and make sure you get a piece of stem with each tuber, otherwise they won't grow next   123 year. It should be noted, however, that dahlias don't have to be lifted every year as long as they are in well-drained soil. I have a friend who leaves hers in year after year.

After all the tubers and corms are dry, dust them with either a bulb dust that incorporates a fungicide, or powdered sulphur. Place a little in a paper bag along with some of the bulbs, then shake them up and down a couple of times to get an even coating. They are now ready to be placed fairly close together in a deep wooden seed flat or sturdy cardboard carton buried in dry peat. When doing this, it is very important to label colours and varieties for next season. Store the box in a cool, dry, frost-free area, such as an unheated room, a garage or a crawl-space.

Other plants that need protection are fuchsias, tibouchinas, marguerites and pelargoniums. None of these plants actually have a dormant period in their native habitat but are more likely to go through a drought period at some stage in the year. Without drought, they'll just keep on growing, and if you have a cool greenhouse or sun room that doesn't drop below about 7°C (45°F) at night, you can simply prune them back and bring them in for the winter, where they will keep gently growing all winter long.

Most of the plants mentioned above can take a little frost, with the exception of tibouchina, and all can be overwintered if they're well buried in a trench. In the milder coastal areas they can be overwintered outside by planting in well-drained soil and building a chicken wire cage around them. The cage should be large enough to cover the whole area and high enough to cover the plants with about 60 centimetres (2 feet) of dry leaves. It should be stressed that the leaves must be dry and lightly packed, to allow air to circulate. Tie plastic over the top to keep out the rain, but leave the sides open. If it is totally enclosed, you'll get instant compost.

When using the trench method, reduce the size of the branched head of tree fuchsias by pruning back by two-thirds, and trim the root area the same way. Bush fuchsias, pelargoniums and marguerites can all be pruned back two-thirds, but be careful with the marguerites— leave some of the small branched growth. If they are pruned back to the hard woody stem they won't shoot out again the following spring.

124

Choose a site for the trench in the rainshadow of a building, where the soil won't waterlog. Most homes have such places under the eaves. Make a trench about 45 centimetres (18 inches) deep and lay the plants on their sides close together (it doesn't matter if they touch). Label each plant and cover them with some peat, filling in with soil to the original level, and mark the area well. You won't have to worry about them at all until you lift them next February or March. At that time they should be repotted in fresh soil and kept on a bright window ledge until planting-out time in April.

Tender bulbous plants like lilies and agapanthus can be protected successfully by using the chicken-wire tent. Place the wire around the plant and secure it with bamboo canes or sticks threaded through the wire and pushed into the soil. Fill the cage form with dry fallen leaves or dry fern fronds, a natural blanket that has the added advantage of enriching the soil with humus by next spring.

This method can be used to protect small shrubs like camellia, nandina and fatsia—especially if this is their first winter in the garden. Larger mature shrubs can be protected by wrapping, but whatever you do, don't use plastic as when temperatures fluctuate condensation tends to build up, causing fungus disease and eventual rotting. Open material like burlap is an ideal protector, allowing air to circulate and creating a pocket insulation effect.

Last but not least, I have to say that we North American gardeners are the tidiest gardeners in the world and usually take away all the dead leaves and twigs that are winter protection for many plants. Please leave your garden untidy for the winter. Dead leaves are nature's blanket and if taken away, winter damage is certain.

Harvesting and Storing Vegetables

Fall in the garden always conjures up the smell of bonfires, and an abundance of leaves and other good things for the compost. This is the transition time, when we put the garden to bed for winter, plant bulbs for the spring, and harvest and store the fruits of our labours in the vegetable garden.

Potatoes are a favourite crop with many home gardeners. While many gardeners grow potatoes just for the delight of eating new potatoes fresh from the ground, there are some later-maturing varieties that can be kept very well through the winter. Lift them when the green tops begin to show signs of dying back and try to choose a dry, settled spell of weather, because potatoes are best left in the sun to dry for a couple of hours (no longer, as they'll start to turn green and once this happens they are toxic and inedible).

Traditionally potatoes were stored in wooden boxes or seed flats, but I've found that large, plastic, open-sided storage containers work really well for vegetables and are reusable year after year. When the potatoes are thoroughly dry, place them in containers alternately with layers of cardboard or several sheets of newspaper. Don't include any damaged potatoes as they'll cause the whole lot to rot. When the bins are full, put them into a cool, dark, frost-free place, like a shed.

Onions can be brought in this month also. Bend the green tops over to hasten the ripening process, and when they start to yellow, lift the onions and lay them on their sides in the sun, turning them occasionally for three or four days to complete the ripening. Put them under cover at night or if it rains. When they are completely dry, hang them in bunches of ten or so from the ceiling of a shed or a similar cool place.

Carrots and beets can be left in the ground provided your soil is well drained. We used to cover the rows with a layer of dry autumn leaves to protect them from frost, scraping a few leaves away to lift the vegetables as needed. This would not work in a poorly drained situation, so if that's the case, or if the ground will freeze in your area, lift carrots and

126

beets around the end of October. Cut off the tops about 5 centimetres (2 inches) above the root and store each crop separately in boxes of dry peat or sand in a cool, frost-free place.

On the coast we can look forward to vegetables that are left in the ground, such as celery, celeriac, parsnips, leeks, rutabagas, winter cabbages and brussels sprouts, all of which taste much better after a frost or two. Not all the province has the right growing conditions for these winter vegetables, but there is always some way of growing yourself some winter greens. First let's deal with the more well-known vegetables that those of us in the milder climates can grow.

Celery is not grown as widely here as it should be, yet we have an ideal climate for it. An excellent way of blanching celery uses 1-litre (1-quart) milk cartons with the bottoms cut out and the tops fully opened. Place them over the plants in July and when harvest time comes around, the celery will be clean and white.

With any of the winter vegetables, particularly brussels sprouts, it is important to keep yellowing and dead leaves picked off around the base of the plants. Better air circulation helps cut down the risk of fungus diseases and rotting, both quite common in a moist climate. Brussels sprouts are much hardier than many of us would believe—I have seen them growing in gardens in Kelowna and the Kootenays. If you've never tried them before, make a note to do so next year; the seed is sown around June. Not only will they provide several feeds throughout the winter, the tops and sides make excellent eating in the spring.

Another vegetable you might try over winter is endive, or winter lettuce, but to be successful with this crop you'll need a cold frame or cool greenhouse. If you don't have a garden, you can still grow vegetables for sandwiches right on your windowsill. One of the easiest crops to grow is curled cress, which is eaten in the seedling stage. It can be grown on several layers of wet paper towel in a large shallow dish.

When the seed is first sown it should be kept dark and checked daily for water. On the second day it will usually have sprouted, and then the dish should be placed in good light. Provided it never dries out, you should be able to harvest fresh greens for salad or sandwiches in three to four days.

127

You can also grow other beans for fresh sprouts, and there are some really nice inexpensive bean sprouters around in health food stores and garden shops. It is important to have a well-designed bean sprouter, as the water needs to be changed daily for success.

Herbs and other small vegetables can be grown under lights. So you see that the dark days of winter don't mean that you can't have fresh, home-grown produce—you just have to change your methods to suit nature's plan.

Composting

I have said it before and I will say it again: you cannot overdo the amount of organic material you add to the soil. It not only improves the quality of your plants but retains moisture too, and it is the secret to the success of any of the great gardens of the world. This time of year, as the leaves start to fall, is a great time to plan on using them, along with all your other garden waste.

The secrets to good compost-making are moisture, nitrogen (to speed up decomposition), and air. My friend, Peter Chan, who is well known for his books and lectures, always puts a layer of twigs in the bottom of his compost, and a pipe with holes punched in it down through the middle. He bases this on the method Chinese farmers used—covering their compost piles with wet mud and sticking bamboo canes through the pile to get much-needed air to the centre of the compost.

It is very important when making compost to chop up whatever you are using into pieces small enough to decompose quickly. Since leaves are abundant right now, I'll use them as an example. Many times first-year gardeners pile up large leaves like those of the big-leafed maple, expecting great compost next season, only to find in the spring that none of the leaves have decomposed, but are perfectly preserved in layers and as tough as ever.

One way to chop up the leaves is to run a mower over them several times before adding them to the compost. Or wait until a few cars have run over the leaves in the street; they make prime composting material. If you are an organic gardener and are worried about the lead content from street leaves, a study carried out by the University of Washington found that the amount is minimal and is leached out by the winter rains.

The best site for compost making is near the vegetable garden, and it should get sun for at least half of the day. If you have the space, build three bins side by side. One is used for the initial gathering, the other for turning half-ready material into, and the third for useable compost.

Some people construct a permanent cement base, but in most areas of B.C. the hardpan or subsoil is quite near the surface, and if you dig down to it, it will make a perfect permanent base at no cost to you. Cedar is the best wood for building the structure. Make the back 3 metres (9 feet) long, so that each bin will be 1 metre (3 feet) wide. The sides, partitions and height should be 1 metre (3 feet), making each bin a square metre (square yard) in size.

All the siding and partition boards should be fixed so that there are air gaps of at least 5 centimetres (2 inches) between each, to allow for good air circulation. I would strongly recommend that the front retainer boards be removeable by sliding them up and out. This will allow you to work easily with the compost.

Start off with a 15-centimetre (6-inch) layer of chopped up material. Whenever I do this I think of my old head gardener who used to say, "Look after the edges and corners and the middle will look after itself." It is sound advice; try it and you'll see. When the first layer is in place, sprinkle it with bone-meal. If the material is on the dry side, add some water before applying the fertilizer, then cover with a layer of soil 5 centimetres (2 inches) deep. Once the first bin is full, cover it with a layer of plastic to keep the fall rains from leaching out the nitrogen.

In three weeks, you can turn the entire contents of the first box into the second. This disturbance hastens the rotting process. Now you can start all over again with the first bin. Three weeks later, turn the middle bin into the last one, where it will soon become useable compost.

If you don't have room for such elaborate structures, there are many good methods for compost-making that suit a small space. I have a friend who makes very good compost in large black plastic garbage bags that are carefully hidden behind a dense planting of shrubs. When I was involved in garden judging, one contestant had an underground compost area hidden by a small deck. There were a few largish but easy to move pots of annuals standing on the deck, which was hinged and could be easily lifted. Whenever new waste was added it was cut into very small pieces.

Another way of making compost in your vegetable garden is the trench method. As soon as your late crops have been harvested, dig a trench that spans the width of your garden, about 60 centimetres (2 feet) wide and deep. Then as the leaves drop and other garden waste, such as dahlia tops and old annuals, accumulates, chop them all up and place them in the trench. When the trench is one-quarter full, sprinkle some ammonium sulphate or powdered bone-meal over the top and cover it with a 5-centimetre (2-inch) layer of soil, just as in the bins. Add more compost material, repeating this procedure, until the trench is full. Then pile the leftover soil on top and open up another trench. By the end of November most of your vegetable patch will have been dug.

At U.B.C. we experimented with a prefabricated compost maker called "Soil Saver." It sells for around $123.00. It did produce useable compost in eight weeks, using green waste such as annual weeds, lower old leaves from cabbages and so on. But there is no reason it couldn't be used for fall and winter composting too. Again, material was well cut up before being added to the pile.

Seaweed makes the best compost. Layered with the regular waste from your garden, it will produce compost very quickly.

If you have somewhat large shrub beds or bush and tree fruit-growing areas in your garden, and you don't have time to make compost, simply mulch those areas with chopped-up leaves to a maximum depth of 15 centimetres (6 inches). Chopping the leaves will decrease the likelihood of the wind blowing them around, and will speed up the decomposition process. By next spring, it should be useful humus for your garden.

To sum up, don't waste what nature is providing at this time of year. It will improve your garden, not just for next season, but for many seasons ahead.

Fall Care of Houseplants

While many of our gardens are still looking good, I think it is fair to say that at this time of year, our attention turns to indoor plants again.

The first priority for houseplants during the shorter days of fall and winter is to make sure they get as much of the available daylight as possible. While it is hard on your plants to be on a south-facing window ledge during the summer months, this is fine now as the sun is too weak to burn. One of the main problems with a window ledge is that usually there is a heat source just below it, and the dry air can cause severe leaf drop and brown tips on the leaves. To help overcome the problem, place each pot in a saucer which is at least 3 centimetres (1½ inches) larger than the pot base. Fill the saucer with pebbles or small rocks and add water to just below the surface of the pebbles. (If you collect the rocks from outdoors, put them in a bucket and pour boiling water over them to sterilize them before using.) Stand your pots on top of the pebbles and make sure that the water level is maintained. The water will evaporate, rising up through the leaves and branches of your plant and supplying a constant source of humidity.

The other problem with placing plants on window ledges is draughts, particularly at night. If it turns cold or windy, any plants that are between your drapes and the glass can be adversely affected. Draught damage to tropical plants produces deformed new growth, so it is safest to move your plants into the room before closing the drapes at night. 131

If heat and draughts are a problem in your house, you might want to install some grow-lights. They are a special kind of light that is as close to sunlight as possible. They can be bought as regular light bulbs that fit any kind of socket, so that if you have plants on an end table, a grow-light bulb can be used in an end-table lamp. The important thing to note about grow-lights is that they should be close to the plant—no more than 60 centimetres (2 feet) away—to be of benefit, and they should be on at least ten hours a day. Whether your plants are near a window or artificial light, they will tend to grow toward the light source, making them lopsided. Turn them at least once a month (I turn mine weekly at this time of year.)

Once the house temperature is raised, plants dry out more quickly, so check for moisture more often. There are fancy battery-operated meters you can get, but if you have been growing plants for awhile you will have adopted other methods, like lifting each pot to feel its weight; usually if it's light, it needs a drink. The other well-tried technique is to stick a finger into the soil up to the first knuckle. Often the soil can look dry but be really moist below.

When you water, make sure that you thoroughly soak the soil all the way through, so that the excess comes out of the drainage holes in the bottom. Most plants, with the exception of flowering ones, like to have a good drink and then be allowed to almost dry out between waterings. Flowering plants like to be kept moist at all times. But remember that no plant enjoys sitting in excess water for more than fifteen minutes. After this amount of time, pour the excess off, as overwatering is one of the biggest killers of houseplants.

Large plants tend to get dusty during the winter and will thoroughly enjoy a lukewarm shower. I stress lukewarm, as once I told a friend to put his rubber plant in the shower and he did, but it was a hot one! It killed the plant down one side, so do be careful with the temperature.

Many houseplant books claim that plants don't need feeding during the winter. This really isn't true, especially if your plants are in a room that is heated to around 23°C (73°F) and has good light. Under these conditions, plants will continue to grow, albeit more slowly. I feel that the lower-nitrogen plant foods—something like liquid seaweed or liquid 6-8-6—are better for the winter months. For fall and winter feeding, reduce the dilution to less than half of the recommended amount and feed only once a month.

The exception to this is the Christmas cactus, if you're trying to get it to bloom for the holidays. Keep it in an east-facing window, and start feeding it every other week with one of the no-nitrogen fertilizer, such as 0-15-14, which will encourage many flower buds. While they are forming, don't let the plant dry out, or they will drop off very quickly. It is also wise not to move the plant around too much, especially after the buds form. With a bit of luck, you should have a colourful living table centre during the holiday season.

Fall Colour

When the weather is dry in autumn, the fall colour can be spectacular. Of course, we don't get the brilliant reds in our native trees like they do in eastern Canada, but the golden hues of our own native maples are very pleasing. And throughout British Columbia we have an excellent opportunity to plant a wide range of trees and shrubs in our home gardens, which can give many colourful showings at this time of year.

One of the hardiest and showiest of shrubs is the winged spindleberry (*Euonymus alatus*), which is also sometimes referred to as burning bush. At maturity it reaches about 2 metres (6 feet) in height and width, but in a garden situation it can be kept pruned to the desired size. The leaves are small but brilliant red at this time of the year. In fact, they are so red that they're hard to look at on bright, sunny days. Once the leaves have dropped, the angled branches are just as interesting, and great for flower arrangements. They are particularly pretty after a first snowfall as the snow lodges in all the ridges, emphasizing the shape.

133

There are many small trees suitable for the home garden, and probably the best known is Japanese maple. But if you live on the coast, you might consider a fall and winter flowering cherry (*Prunus subhirtella autumnalis*) which has good colour at this time and is followed by masses of little cherry blossoms November through January.

Another very good small tree for home gardens in the more temperate areas is *Stewartia psuedocamellia*. Botanical names can be difficult to deal with but unless a plant is widely known or grown, it has no common name. For this particular one, "false camellia" would work very well. The name comes from the flower, which when it blooms in June or July looks exactly like a single white camellia. In the fall the leaves range from yellow to orange to bright red, so that on dull days the tree almost looks illuminated. Another nice thing is that the leaves stay on for quite a few weeks. The tree grows to a height of 4 metres (12 feet) and isn't too wide, making a nice feature tree in a lawn area. Once the leaves have dropped, the dark brown seed pods can be seen, and they make the tree interesting over the winter months.

Mountain ash is a hardy tree that gives good fall colour with a brilliant display of red berries. Very soon after the first frost the berries start to ferment, and then you can see many a drunken robin around the boulevards. 'Joseph Rock' is a beautiful yellow-berried variety of mountain ash, and you can see a speciment of it in VanDusen Gardens. Beauty berry (*Callicarpa japonica*) is a bush with unusual berries. From a distance the berries appear to be a haze of purple-mauve blossoms, quite out of character with other colours associated with this season. Another more common shrub for the coastal area is firethorn (*Pyracantha*), which is invaluable as it thrives in both sun and shade.

There is a fine relative of our native huckleberry, *Pernyetta mucronata*, which comes from South America and is available in several different forms. 'Alba' has white berries, 'Coccinea' scarlet berries, and 'Rosea' pink. Pernettya is a low-growing shrub, great for using on difficult slopes even near salt water, and its sharp pointed evergreen leaves keep unwanted animals and others out of your garden.

There are also some lovely vines that provide good colour in the fall. The old Sylvia Hotel on English Bay in Vancouver always looks so glorious when the Virginia creeper turns. This vine is hardier than you might think, so those in the interior should give it some garden space, particularly if you have an old stump to cover or a fence that could use some softening up. Another vine, also called Virginia creeper, is *Parthenocissus netirophylla*, which has clusters of five leaves. I remember several of those vines planted outside the reception area at Lake Louise. They leafed out around mid-June and were always in full colour when the first snow came early in September, so that proves how hardy they are.

It is possible in temperate regions of the province to plant these specimens now, but in colder areas, I would wait until spring.

NOVEMBER

CHAPTER ELEVEN

Winter Digging and Clean-up

Very few of us actually do winter digging anymore, as most people prefer to do their digging in the spring, just before planting up the garden. But if you have heavy soil, like clay, digging at this time can be beneficial, as the winter freezing and thawing will help to break it down into a nice friable tilth, and annual weeds like chickweed, groundsel, and euphorbia can be totally eradicated from your garden if completely buried at this time of year. If these arguments have convinced you, now through to the end of January is a good time to do your winter digging.

Digging should not be as intimidating as it sounds. If you have a large garden, you don't have to do it all in one go; you can start this weekend and do a row or two at a time over the next three months. Of course, in the vegetable garden there will be a lot of old weeds and vegetables left around, all of which make excellent material to dig in.

Traditionally a vegetable garden was dug two spades deep, commonly called double digging. However, in some of the hardpan areas of the province, you may be lucky to get one spade's depth. In any case, first take out a trench one spade's depth and perhaps a tad wider all

136

across one end of your garden. As you dig, put the soil directly into a wheelbarrow and take it down to the other end of your vegetable patch. This soil will be used to fill in the last trench once you have finished digging.

If you are able to double dig, scrape some weeds, old vegetables, and garden waste into the trench, along with some manure if you can get it, or seaweed if you're near the coast. Then turn it under a further spade's depth. If you can't double dig, then just open another trench and use that soil to fill in the first trench. When you get to the last trench at the other end of the garden, your wheelbarrow of soil will be waiting to fill it in.

By the way, it is quite safe to dig in fresh manure at this time of the year, as the winter rains will leach out the salts and other burning elements, leaving behind wonderful humus for the roots to get into in the spring.

For digging, I recommend a long-handled spade. Being of English background I used to frown at long-handled shovels, but I've since learned that they're much kinder to your back. No matter which you choose, however, and this goes for all your tools, it is very important to keep them clean. Always wash them off when you have finished with them, then dry them and wipe them with an oily rag. They won't rust and will make gardening so much more enjoyable.

If you still have a little garden clean-up to do, stand back and have a look first. All those dead and unsightly looking leaves will make a wonderful protective winter blanket should we get severe weather, so don't take it all away. Go ahead and trim plants that are getting in the way, but with perennials like Michaelmas daisies and delphiniums, leave about 30 centimetres (12 inches) of stem on. They can be trimmed back next spring when new growth starts to appear. Gardeners in the interior, where they are assured of good winter snow cover, can cut things back more drastically, but as weather is so unpredictable, I would still leave major clean-up until spring.

Dormancy and Pruning

Pruning is such a difficult activity to explain. You almost need to have a tree in front of you to explain it properly. And in a province as vast as ours there are two schools of thought on the right time of year for pruning fruit trees.

In the Okanagan the pruning is done after the worst of the winter freezes have passed, February or March, and for a very good reason. If a hard pruning was carried out before an extreme cold spell, it is quite possible that some of the wood could be permanently damaged. But in the more temperate regions of B.C., it's not a bad idea to start pruning as soon as all the leaves have dropped from your apples, pears, plums, and other fruit trees. At this stage, the trees have essentially gone dormant. Anytime between now and the end of January is fine for pruning on the coast.

The basic principles of pruning a fruit tree are to remove dead or inward-growing and crossing branches; to allow for good air circulation throughout the tree, which in turn permits the sun to get at flowers and fruit and makes harvesting easier; and to maintain the appropriate shape for the tree. It is important to remember with young trees that along with pruning for fruit production, you are also shaping the future of your tree. So be very careful before you cut anything off! Before doing any pruning stand well back and look at that tree from all sides.

When pruning ornamental trees and shrubs, you try to leave as much of the new flower-bearing wood on as possible, in order to get a good showing of blossoms in the spring. When pruning fruit trees, you want to keep some of the flower-bearing wood, as it will produce fruit, but you want to keep less of it. That way the tree isn't encouraged to overbear, resulting in lots of small fruit and weakening of the tree. Increasing the sun and air circulation lessens the likelihood of apple scab, powdery mildew, and other fungus-related diseases.

As with all pruning, first remove any deadwood and crossing bran-ches. Crossing branches are the ones that grow back toward the centre of the tree, or rub against another branch.

Next you should familiarize yourself with the difference between a fruit bud and a normal growth bud. Fruit buds are always the fatter ones. Quite often on older established trees, they are in thick clusters on the ends of very short branches called fruiting spurs. Your tree will have many other types of growth, and it is these growths that we need to thin out and reduce in order to let the sun in.

A general rule of thumb when pruning fruit trees is to reduce the leader shoot by one-third (the leader shoot is out on the end of a branch leading to the light) and the lateral or side shoots by two-thirds. When I'm pruning, I try to reduce the lateral shoots to about three or four buds, especially if they don't have any fruiting buds on them, as the drastic approach will often encourage them to become fruiting spurs. Some fruit trees tend to form fruit buds quite a way out on their new growth and these are referred to as tip bearers in the trade. If that is where the fruit is being produced, naturally you will leave those shoots longer.

With the topmost leader of a young tree make a cut at a 45-degree angle just above a strong-looking bud, sloping the cut back away from the bud. For side shoots, make your cuts above outward facing buds. This way you will cut down on the potential for shoots growing in to-ward the centre of the tree.

The small branches growing into the centre of the tree, even if they look like fruit-bearing wood, should be cut out at this stage. The longer they are left, the larger and harder they will be to remove. When cutting larger branches, I like to use some kind of pruning paint. It can be any regular brown or green paint that you might have left over from a paint-ing project.

On older established trees, the principles are the same but you will have to be more careful about knocking off too many flower buds. If an old tree has been neglected there may be some larger branches to be removed. But assess them well from afar before and after each cut. Pruning can be a wee bit too therapeutic for some people, and after be- 139 ing up in the tree, cutting away, they finally get down and stand back only to find there is nothing left.

It's all right to be a little timid when you first start pruning, but experienced pruners often take a different approach. When I was in training in horticulture my old head gardener would come by after we had pruned the large old apple trees in the orchard and throw his trilby hat up through the branches. If it could go up and fall back down without getting caught up, he was satisfied. But if it got caught, we had to go back and prune a little more.

For any pruning it is important to have a good, clean, sharp pair of pruners and a pruning saw. Many fungal and bacterial diseases are spread from one tree to another by dirty pruning tools, so always wash the blades of your pruners immediately after pruning one tree and before moving on to the next. I usually wash mine in a household bleach or disinfectant. After washing, dry them and rub them with an oily rag, which keeps them from rusting.

Those of you with pears will know that it is a little difficult to open up the centre of the tree, as all new growth on pears tends to go straight up into the air. To train a young pear into shape and open up the branch network, wrap twine around each branch and anchor it to a peg in the ground. This twine should stay in place for a season so that the wood has a chance to ripen and harden into the open shape permanently.

On older trees I have seen sticks used to wedge branches apart for a season. They stay in place because a little v is cut in each end. Then they are also removed at the end of the growing season.

Remember it is fun to prune. Don't get carried away and stand back now and then to assess the shape of your tree. The *RHS Practical Dictionary of Gardening* has one volume that deals just with pruning. I think it is still the best book available, with step-by-step illustrated instructions. And the book comes in a transparent waterproof cover, so you can just open it to the page you want, slip it in its cover, and take it to your fruit tree for easy reference.

When the pruning is done and all the old fruit is knocked off, wash the fruit trees with lime sulphur. It is a fungicide, and used at 50 millilitres (2 ounces) per litre (quart) of water it will help eradicate overwintering spores of peach leaf curl, pear and apple scab, and black knot on plums. It will also kill moss and lichens on the branches. The application is quite strong and should only be used on dormant trees at this strength. For readers in the interior, pruning and spraying should be carried out in the thaw period in the spring, any time before buds begin to break.

Growing Herbs and Greens under Lights

Herbs like parsley, chives, and thyme can continue to grow in coastal gardens right into November, and with a mild winter, it is even possible to go into the garden during the holiday season to pick some herbs for that good homemade turkey stuffing. However, if you want to be absolutely sure that you have herbs all winter long, then lift some of your plants and bring them into your cool greenhouse or cold frame.

Not everything transplants well and perhaps the least easy to move is parsley. But if you do it after a rain and try to get as much soil on the roots as possible, chances are that it will continue to grow moderately well over the next three months or so.

If your greenhouse is standing directly on open ground, then you might want to plant the freshly lifted herbs directly into the soil. First consider whether or not you want to incorporate artificial light into growing your herbs. Artificial light will certainly make them produce more leaves, because although bringing them into a warm environment helps, growth will still slow down because of lack of light. By providing artificial light, the plant is fooled into thinking that either the growing season has been extended or spring is just around the corner.

If you decide to opt for the lights, pot up the plants; it will be easier to   141 install the lights over a bench than to hang them close to the ground.

In a greenhouse, where you already have good natural light, it isn't necessary to have grow-lights; a combination of a cool white and a warm white fluorescent tube hung about 30 centimetres (12 inches) above the plants works well. The lights should be on at least twelve hours a day, and thirteen hours would more closely simulate spring or summer. If you can be there every day and are good at remembering to turn lights on and off, then you've got it made. If you're like me, you will need to install an inexpensive timer for peace of mind.

In a cold frame it isn't as easy to add lights, but the cold frame can still work quite well if placed against a sheltered south- or west-facing wall, providing there are no prolonged cold spells.

When you're ready to sow, any lettuce seed you have left over from the summer should work, but there are recommended varieties for winter growing. 'Winter Density', 'Grand Rapids', and 'Green Ice' are three. The first is a romaine-type while the latter two are fast-maturing leaf lettuce. It will be almost impossible to find seed of these in garden centres at this time of the year, so make a note to order some seed in the spring for next year.

When growing herbs in a greenhouse or cold frame, use regular garden soil or patio pot mix. But indoors it is strongly recommended to use a good sterile potting mix, so that you don't bring in pests and diseases.

Sow about six lettuce seeds per pot and barely cover them with the mix. Keep them in a warm dark place (such as the kitchen counter, covered with black plastic) until they've germinated, keeping them moist, of course. As soon as they've germinated, they are placed under the lights. They are ready for harvesting when the leaves are about 45 centimetres (18 inches) in length. To keep a constant supply, sow two pots at a time at three-day intervals.

Apartment dwellers may have trouble growing herbs inside if the temperature in the building is too hot. Any herbs or greens will last only a short while, unless you can keep them near an open window. If you have an extra room that you can keep cool, 10° to 16°C (50 to 60°F) by day and no lower than 5°C (41°F) at night, put up a bank of four lights (either grow-lights or the fluorescent tubes mentioned earlier) over an area about the size of a four-seater dining table. If possible hang them on chains from hooks in the ceiling, so that the lights can be raised as the plants grow.

If the room doesn't get much natural light, keep the lights on twelve hours a day. With the artificial and natural light, correct temperature, and good air circulation, the growing conditions will be similar to spring and you should be able to grow winter lettuce, spinach, and other quick-growing green-leafed plants. If you have perfect conditions, you might try some early tiny carrots or even fast-maturing beets. With the latter, if the bottoms don't develop you can always eat the tops as greens.

If you have the space, time, and inclination, by all means grow some herbs this winter. Although it is quite expensive to grow plants under lights, and in the city we have access to good fresh produce all winter long, it is delightful to pick your own fresh greens right when you need them. For more information on growing winter plants, a trip to your local library will provide a cross-section of excellent books on the subject.

Your Garden in Winter

No matter where you live in British Columbia, there are certain trees and shrubs that can be planted to give interesting shapes and bark colour all winter long. We are, of course, spoiled in the milder regions of the province, so let's start with the possibilities for those in the colder areas. Of course, you won't be planting now—that will wait for spring—but you can be planning at this time.

Red osier dogwoods are always a good choice for areas where there is a winter snow cover that isn't so deep that it buries the shrub. As the name implies, the stems are a beautiful red colour all year long, but they look particularly spectacular against the white backdrop of snow. 143

Botanical names can be so annoying to remember, but if you want a really good red-stemmed form, you'll need to ask for *Cornus alba sibirica*, commonly known as Siberian dogwood. There is also a form that has showy yellow twigs in winter, *Cornus stolonifera flaviramea*. Perhaps it is known as the yellow osier dogwood. In both cases, to get the best coloured stems in winter they should be pruned back almost to the ground early in the spring, just before new growth starts.

There are also two members of the spindleberry family worth growing for winter interest. The first is the spindleberry bush (*Euonymus europeas*), which is really more of a shrubby tree. It has fascinating berries in the fall. They are in brilliant pink clusters, and when ripe they split open to reveal an orange seed inside. In the colder regions I have seen these berries frozen on the tree all winter, giving a pleasant colour in an otherwise bleak landscape. The twigs are a pleasant bright green all winter. A shrubby member of this group is the winged spindleberry, which is discussed on page 133. Its curiously shaped ridged branches have a fairyland appearance when snow gets caught on them.

If silver twigs are a favourite with you, then you must grow the 'Autumn Olive', known botanically as *Eleagnus umbellata*. It has silver foliage that drops in the fall, when the silver bark comes into its own. Some hard pruning early in the spring will encourage more young wood to develop for better bark colour next fall.

In milder areas of the province a great number of interesting trees and shrubs can be grown for winter enjoyment. 'Harry Lauder's Walking Cane' (*Corylus avellana contorta*) is a contorted form of the filbert tree that we are all familiar with. Unfortunately the contortion is carried in the foliage in the growing season, giving the tree a diseased look, but it's all worth it once the foliage has dropped off and the curious curled branches become fully visible. The branches are sought after for Japanese flower arranging. I have a friend who has planted one in a courtyard garden that is seen from the house all winter. At the base she has installed an outdoor spotlight that shines up through the branches during these dreary winter evenings. The effect is beautiful.

A fine small tree for a home garden in milder areas is the snake-bark maple (*Acer davidii*). As the name suggests, the bark is marked with an almost regular grey and green diamond-shaped marking. It makes a striking addition to a winter garden.

On the lower mainland coast and in the Gulf Islands, several winter flowering shrubs will grow. Winter jasmine, whose golden yellow flowers have blossomed already, will carry on during frost-free weather right through until the end of February.

The autumn- and winter-flowering plum causes quite a stir when it's first seen. As soon as the leaves have dropped in early November it starts to blossom and carries on through the winter. It makes a good small garden tree. For more information on winter-flowering shrubs, see page 7.

If you don't have winter colour in your garden now, make a note to plant one or two specimens next year, so you can enjoy your garden year-round.

Winter Watch

The onset of winter weather means that all gardeners need to keep a weather watch. We never quite know what the weather will be like, particularly in the more temperate areas of the province.

Heavy wet snows can be quite harmful to the shape of conifers and newly planted trees, particularly those with very bushy branches. With evergreens such as upright junipers and ornamental cedars that are multi-trunked, it's a good idea to tie the branches in loosely to the trunk with some strong twine. Spiral it around the whole body of the tree so that it is loosely parcelled, and it will hold it nicely in shape no matter what the weather. Don't forget to make a note on your calendar to remove the twine next March or April.

It is important that small, newly planted trees be staked against strong winter winds, especially if you live in an exposed area. Place three stakes around the tree, leaning them in toward the tree at the top. Wrap the trunk where the stakes touch with some burlap or similar material to prevent rubbing.

In interior areas where mice damage the bark by eating it under the snow, you can get a heavy spiralled type of plastic material to wrap around the lower trunk, or you can recycle plastics such as pieces of old downpipe or bleach bottles by slitting one side and clamping them around the trunk. Again, remember to remove them in the spring when the snow has melted.

Bush roses should not be pruned until February or March, but large varieties, like 'Queen Elizabeth', tend to whip around in the winter winds and work themselves loose in the soil. To prevent this, you can prune them back by two-thirds to one-half right now, to remove the bulk and make winter wind damage less likely. Interior readers can help their roses through the winter by mounding up soil around the bases of their bushes, much like hilling potatoes, which protects the lower growth buds from being frozen.

In the warmer areas where it is possible to grow borderline hardy plants such as figs, kiwi fruit and loquats, build a chicken wire cage about 30 centimetres (12 inches) from the wall which extends from the top to the bottom of the tree and fill the cavity with dry leaves, bracken, or straw. It will guarantee the plant coming through the winter. Do the same with newly planted shrubs, such as banksian rose, raphiolepsis, and *Fatsia japonica*, that were grown south of the border and imported to garden shops this spring.

Some of the plants we grow in alpine gardens don't like the rain and should be protected from it by plastic cloches. Bend wire or canes parallel to each other on each side of the plant to form an arc, then stretch heavy-gauge clear plastic over the top. Bury the excess in the soil to hold it firm and leave the ends open for good circulation. Incidentally, this works well for helleborus, or Christmas roses, as it keeps the rain from splashing the blossoms and lengthens the flower stems, making them more suitable for cut flowers in the home.

Exposed apartment balconies are difficult to work with when overwintering plants, especially if they are north-facing. One method that works amazingly well is to put all the patio containers inside a large cardboard carton and then fill in the gaps with crumpled-up newspapers. I've also seen old styrofoam picnic coolers used for storing borderline hardy plants. It works in reverse of its summertime use and really keeps the frost out.

Once you've taken care of all these winterizing tasks, you might want to turn your attention ahead to the next growing season. Now is a good time to plan and make any new wooden patio planters or hanging baskets you might need next year.

Expensive yellow or red cedar are the best woods to use, but virtually any hardwood that is treated with a good preservative and is treated over the years will last fifteen to twenty years. A good minimum size for planters is 45 centimetres (18 inches) square and 30 centimetres (12 inches) deep. Hanging baskets this size are also practical, as they don't dry out as fast, providing you have strong enough hooks.

If the planters are for an open patio exposed to rain it is important to have adequate drainage either in the bottom or in the sides close to the bottom. You need about four holes approximately 3 centimetres (1¼ inches) in diameter for a 45-square-centimetre (18-square-inch) box.

Once they are built, treat them two or three times with a wood preservative containing copper napthenate. Some readers will be horrified at this recommendation, particularly if the containers are to be used for growing food crops. However, if the preservative is applied early enough and the planters are completely dry well before April, there won't be a problem. Copper napthenate is only toxic when applied to plants in a liquid form.

For ideas on plans and designs for planters, you should be able to find books at the library, either in the gardening or the do-it-yourself sections.

If you have established planters that are empty, now is the time to empty the soil into large plastic bags and bring the planters into the basement or shed, where they can dry out over the next six weeks. Then they can be treated with preservative as well. However, don't apply this method to half-barrels that were used for aging alcohol. They will just shrink and fall apart if emptied, and they don't need to be treated, as the alcohol will preserve the oak for years.

DECEMBER

CHAPTER TWELVE

Planting up
Your Own Gifts

Homemade holiday gifts are always fun to make, and I believe they give a lot more pleasure to the receiver. You can do a lot with some inexpensive houseplants—either flowering or green—and some attractive baskets and containers. If you are on a limited budget, you can make wonderful displays using the smaller, less expensive plants.

Rather than purchasing the large poinsettias, get the small individual ones that are in 10-centimetre (4-inch) pots. At the same time, get a selection of easy-to-grow plants, such as peperomia, ivy or creeping fig. You'll need a bag of potting soil and some small baskets—around 30 centimetres (12 inches) in diameter or a little smaller.

As with all repotting, water the plants well in advance and moisten the potting soil so that it sticks lightly together when squeezed. Line each basket with two or three layers of plastic. I use black plastic garbage bags because they are easier to hide. Next place a shallow layer of broken styrofoam cups or other material in the bottom for drainage and add a sprinkling of crushed charcoal to keep the soil sweet.

148   Tap your plants out of their pots and arrange them nicely in the bas-

ket. If the basket is to be appreciated from all sides, then varying heights all around will be fine. If it is to be seen from one side only, put the taller plants to the back.

Once the plants are in place, gently fill in the gaps between the root balls with the extra potting mix, then carefully tuck in any black plastic that might be showing. If you live in an area where moss is plentiful, hide the surface of the soil and the plastic with a layer of moss on top. You will be quite pleased with the professional yet natural look this achieves. If it is to be a Christmas present, you can tie a big red bow on the basket.

A nice effect can be achieved using all green plants when you add a spray of cut flowers. To do this, bury a small jar or bottle of water in between the plants when planting. Then when you're finished, stick two or three stems of orchids or spray mums in the bottle. They will look terrific, and when they fade they can be replaced with more cut flowers.

Another gift that is care-free for the recipient and fun for children to make is a terrarium. For instructions on how to make one, see page 5.

If you grew some bulbs for Christmas giving, the first week or two in December is the time to lift them up, so that they are ready to bloom for Christmas. (Directions on repotting and handling of forced bulbs are on page 120.) When potting them for gifts, place three or four to a basket. If you can't get any moss to mask the surface, sow some grass seed on the surface of the potting mix. It will germinate by the time you give the gift, giving the whole basket a spring-like appearance.

Taller bulbs like narcissus and daffodils will already be planted in groups in larger pots, so at this stage, while they are still short, go out into the garden and gather some bushy twigs with your pruners. Try to cut them in lengths just shy of the mature height of the bulbs and push them into the bare spaces of soil between the bulbs. While it will look a little funny to start out, the bulbs will eventually grow up between the twigs, hiding them almost completely but giving them some support.

As for the poinsettia that you have been faithfully putting to bed each night in a dark closet and bringing out each day for the past two months, if it hasn't turned red by now, I have to tell you that it isn't going to. The frustrating thing is that it will probably be red for Easter, but look at it this way: you are keeping the poinsettia growers in business. 149

Gifts for Gardeners

It's that time of year again, and it's time to purchase gifts for your gardening friends. Probably gardeners are the easiest people to get gifts for; who else would be thrilled when you give them a box of fertilizer?

Books are always a good place to start, and a good value along these lines is the series by the Royal Horticultural Society called the *Encyclopaedia of Practical Gardening*, published by Simon and Schuster. There are eight volumes in the series: *Pruning, Propagation, Vegetables, Fruit, Lawns, Pests and Diseases, Growing under Glass*, and *Gardening Techniques*. They are concise, easy to follow, well illustrated, and come packaged for the novice gardener; each one has a heavy clear plastic envelope so you can take it out to the garden with you.

Another delightful book that crossed my desk last year is *The Apple Book*, by Peter Blackburne-Maze, published by Collingridge in the UK. It details the history of apples and lists varieties suitable for the home garden, most of which are available here. The illustrations are charming and informative.

The last book is a very useful volume called *Easy Plants for Difficult Places*—something every garden has. It is written by Geoffrey Smith and published by Hamlin. But there are many great books available, so shop around.

The types of tools gardeners like to receive are things like pruners, as they are fairly expensive and not something you rush out and purchase at the drop of a hat. Wilkinsons are still considered the Cadillac of pruners by some, but Felco pruning shears from Switzerland are a very good value. They are well manufactured, extremely strong, and come in a wide range of prices. If your friend is left-handed, it is possible to get a pair especially for him or her.

Pruning saws are another acceptable gift. There are some really nice models with blades that fold back into their handles, a good safety feature when carrying them up into a tree.

Depending on your price range, there are some wonderful stainless steel tools that cost around $80.00 for a fork or spade. They are extremely well built and balanced and will last the lucky recipient a lifetime.

Other thoughtful gifts are gardener's log books, a place to keep records for future years reflection, nice labels and a waterproof pen, some peat pots to prepare for the spring, or a thermometer. Thermometers are always useful to a gardener who has a greenhouse or cold frame. The best ones are the maximum/minimum type that have a double mercury tube. Two little markers inside the tube stay where the mercury pushes them, recording the maximum and minimum temperatures for the past day or night.

Something like a kneeling pad may not seem glamorous to you, but to gardening friends who spend a lot of time on their knees, weeding or edging, it might be seen as a luxury and perhaps not an item they would buy for themselves.

If you are thinking of houseplants as a gift, consider unusual plants like bromeliades, or air plants. You can take them out of their pots, wrap their roots in moss and attach them to attractive pieces of driftwood. They can be hung in a bathroom or kitchen, where the humidity is high, as long as there is good light. They just need to be misted daily, and the central funnel kept moist at all times, as this is where they get their food and moisture.

Kalanchoes come in many colours ranging from a brilliant Christmas red, through pink, magenta, orange, and yellow. Their native environment is the desert, which makes them slightly more tolerant of hot, dry room conditions. The star-like flowers occur in clusters on the top of the plant, and the leaves are fleshy, like a succulent. They can take a sunny window ledge, and they need to be watered well, so that you see excess moisture draining from the pot. Then tip it away until the plant is almost completely dry before watering again. Kalanchoes are fairly long-lived. After the flowers have faded, cut the flower stems back to the foliage, and repot if necessary. In the summer months, the plant 151 can be put outside in a spot where it gets morning sun and afternoon shade.

Another attractive gift plant for the holiday season is coral berry, *Ardisia crispa*. Its smallish leaves look like evergreen leaves, but the main features are the flowers and berries, which are on the plant at the same time. The bright red berries are plentiful, occurring in a circular fashion all around the plant about 10 centimetres (4 inches) down from the top. The flowers are right at the top and are very white. Coral berry is easy to care for, although it must be kept moist while the berries and flowers are on. It has always surprised me that coral berries haven't been mass-produced for the Christmas season; with a red or green bow, it's hard to imagine a better gift plant.

Another nice gift for someone who is really good with plants is a stag-shorn fern. They come from Queensland, where they grow on the tree trunks, and they can be grown the same way as bromeliades.

If your gardening friend appears to have everything he or she needs, there are always gift certificates, or a year's membership in the garden of your choice. A membership will keep them in touch with the gardening world and give free entry to the garden. And as all public gardens have difficulty raising funds these days, this gift will help the garden to thrive while giving your friend a year's enjoyment.

Christmas Trees and Such

As the big holiday approaches your family will be anxious for you to put the tree up. Before doing so, there are a few things you can do to make your holiday season safer and more enjoyable.

To ensure a really fresh cut tree, you can go to a tree farm and cut your own, but buying from a tree lot can be tricky. The trees have often been cut for quite awhile before they reach the tree lots and are quite dehydrated by the time you take them home. When buying cut trees from a lot, it is strongly recommended that you spray them with a fire retardant before bringing them in the house.

When picking out a live cut tree, try to choose one that still looks a good bright green colour. If you have doubts, bend a needle or two. If they bend easily there's still life in the tree but if they snap in half, the tree is dead and you should look for another one.

Before putting them in the stand, cut off at least 5 centimetres (2 inches) of the stem to encourage the tree to take up some water—warm sugar water sometimes works wonders. Once the tree starts to take up water, you will need to top up the water container daily. This is easy to forget once the holiday season is at its height.

If you prefer a live tree that you can plant out in the garden after Christmas, you should plan on having it in a warm house no longer than the period between Christmas Eve and New Year's Day.

Evergreens are dormant at this time of year, and the sudden burst of heat can fool them into premature growth. This is probably not too harmful in the milder areas of the province, but if you live in the Interior, where it can be quite nippy, the tree could suffer badly when it is put directly out into the garden. If the weather is cold, keep the tree in an unheated garage or shed for a few days before putting it directly outside.

While the live tree is in the house, have it in a container large enough to ensure that the roots are properly watered, and turn the heat down at night—the cooler the better. Miniature lights are best for a live tree, and

153

make sure to only have the lights on when you are at home, as they can dehydrate the tree. This also applies to decorating large indoor Norfolk Island pines or other houseplants.

Decorating your home with live greens can be fun and there is a wealth of material to choose from, especially on the coast. If you can keep the greens in water they will stay fresher looking. I use a product called Oasis, a floral foam that absorbs water and holds it for some time. Florist shops and some garden supply stores carry it, and a standard block cut into four pieces will make four nice arrangements.

Make sure you have your greens cut the appropriate length before sticking them in the soaked foam, as each time you insert a stem it makes a hole. If you are using candles in the arrangements, don't place them directly into the foam, as they use up too much space. Instead, I use a pliable but strong wire to make two hairpin bends about 8 centimetres (3 inches) in length when bent. Holding the two bent wires on either side of the candle base, so that there are four legs about 5 centimetres (2 inches) long extending down from it, carefully tape the wires in place. The candle can then be placed on the Oasis foam by pushing the wires all the way in so that the base of the candle is flush with the surface of the Oasis.

If you don't have any berries to brighten the greens up, add some small red bows or Christmas tree baubles. Cut flowers, such as freesia, also make a nice addition. Once you have finished your arrangement you shouldn't be able to see the base.

A kissing bough hung over your door can be a delightful addition to holiday decorating, and a nice way to welcome all your guests. It can be made from a number of greens, such as holly, ivy, or fir, but it must have a sprig or two of mistletoe in it to make it right.

As a base for this I use a rather large potato, which not only secures the greens but supplies moisture throughout the holidays. Run a wire through the potato and make a bend in the bottom to hold it in place. The wire at the top can be bent over when finished to attach a nice red bow and ribbon for hanging it up.

Cut all your pieces of greens about 10 to 15 centimetres (4 to 6 inches) in length, and when cutting them, make the cuts on an angle so that they are pointed and will stick easily into the potato. First fill it in all over with the softer, easier to handle greens, then add the holly and mistletoe.

Wreaths are always nice to hang on a door, but if you don't have time to make one, a spray of cedar branches highlighted with different and shorter lengths of holly, pine, skimmia or any other interesting berries can be very attractive.

Arrange the boughs flat on a table in a spray, tie them securely with twine, and mask it with a big red bow. Hang with the branches pointing downward and the ribbon trailing down through it. The effect is quite charming and every bit as nice as anything you'll see in a book of decorations.

Having written all this, I realize that none of it is really gardening advice, but greenery and potatoes are from the garden, so I guess that makes it all legitimate.

Caring for Christmas Gift Plants

Houseplants are a popular gift at Christmas, and naturally we all want to keep them healthy and blooming as long as possible.

The most popular Christmas plant is the poinsettia. While it is not difficult to care for, some problems may turn up, especially in a hot, dry room. First, all flowering plants sold at this time of year will have been grown in a greenhouse, where the conditions are just right to produce perfect saleable plants—good light, constant humidity, and the right amount of fertilizer on a regular basis keep the foliage good and healthy. The first priority for the new owner should be to keep the plant in the best light you can offer at this time of year, which means a south- or west-facing window ledge during the day. Keep the potting mix on the moist side, although it is important that it not be waterlogged.

Feed the plant once a week with a weak solution of your favourite liquid fertilizer. To stop the bottom leaves from yellowing and falling off, try to keep the poinsettia in a cooler room at night, and stand the pot on a saucer of pea gravel that has water just below the surface.

Poinsettias keep their coloured bracts for weeks; I've even seen them still on the plant as late as June! But if you plan on keeping your poinsettias for next Christmas, cut them back by two-thirds in late February or early March. It will encourage new bushy growth from the base and keep the plant a more manageable size.

Cyclamen is another favourite plant for giving. It is most essential that cyclamen be kept in cooler conditions if you wish them to last for any length of time. If they can't be kept cool during the day, then it is essential that they be put in a cool garage or like spot overnight. In milder areas of the province, you can even put them outdoors overnight, as long as there is no danger of frost.

Miniature oranges have attractive fruit at this time of year and are often given as gifts, but keeping that fruit on is a major challenge. Never let a fruiting plant dry out at the root, as the first part to suffer is the fruit. By cutting its moisture off, the critical cells between the stem and the fruit dehydrate, which causes the fruit to drop. Don't move the plant around a lot, and try to keep it in a well-lit location for the winter months. Later in the season, when the fruit has dropped and the danger of frost is past, the whole plant can be put outside for the summer, where it will flower and set fruit for the following season.

Christmas cactus are very picky and hate to be moved around. They do best on a table top or window ledge. They also seem to like east-facing situations where they get morning sun and afternoon shade.

Mums are sold year-round now, but are still a popular item at Christmas. They are a good standby plant and quite hard to kill. Pot mums, as you will have observed, are short, but if you keep them to plant out in your garden in the spring, they will spurt up to become four to six times the size they were in the pot. This is because they are treated with a hormone growth retardant in the nursery, which is effective for about six months and then wears off.

Mums and Christmas cactus should both be kept on the moist side while they are blooming. In fact, all flowering and fruiting plants should be kept moist at all times. Lastly, any plant that has come from a nurs-156 ery should be fed once a month with weak liquid fertilizer.

INDEX

Abutilon (flowering maple),
  outside for summer, 85
  in patio pot, 62
Acer davidii (snake bark maple), 144
Actinidia kolmikta, 83
African violet,
  cuttings, 26
Air layering, 94
Aluminum plant, see Pilea
Alyssum, sweet, 67
Amaryllis,
  aftercare, 12
  starting up, 122
Anemone, 118
Annual flowers, 4
  deadheading, 107
  for cutting, 51
  heliotrope, 5
  hibiscus, 4
  matthiola, 5
  mignonette, 5
  nemesia, 4
  nicotiana, 4
  poppy, 4
Aphids,
  black, organic control, 89
  control, 73
  on roses, 86
Apples,
  mildew, 75
Ardisia crispa, 152
Artificial light,
  uses, 35
Asters (Michaelmas daisy),
  annuals for cutting, 51
  divided, 31
Azaleas,
  houseplants, 93
  moving, 20

Babies' tears (helxine), 6
Bachelor's buttons,
  cut flower, 51
  for colour, 67
  sowing time, 51, 58
Balcony gardens, 61
Basil, 39
Beans,
  blackfly, 89
  blossom drop, 105
  broad, sowing, 37
  bush, 89
  bush late cropping, 89
  pole beans, 66
  scarlet runners, 66
Bear berry, see *Arctostaphilos*
Beauty berry, see *Callicarpa japonica*
Bedding plants,
  between spring bulbs, 60
  hardening off, 54, 55
  how to plant, 58
  in containers, 62
  spacing, 58
Beets,
  sowing, 57
  varieties, 57
  winter protection, 126
Begonia,
  mildew, 76
  B.rex from cuttings, 26
  seed sowing, 35
  tuberous lifting and storing, 123
Blackberries, pruning, 15, 111
Black spot, on roses, 87
Blueberries, pruning, 15
Bok choy, 109
Books,
  as gifts, 150
  useful, 33, 46, 140

157

Bottle gardens, 5
Bougainvillea, pruning, 12, 13
Broccoli,
    planting and spacing, 59
    summer sowing, 82
Bromeliades,
    on driftwood, 151
Brown rot on cherries, 74
Brussels sprouts, 4
    crop maintenance, 127
    feeding, 105
    planting and spacing, 59
    where to plant, 89
    winter harvesting time, 127
Bugs and pests, see Pests
Bulbs,
    deep planting, 60
    dust, 124
    forcing, 120
    forcing aftercare, 12
    forced Christmas gardening, 120
    in patio pots, 62, 117
    naturalizing, 117
    planting in pots, 60
    spring aftercare, 59
    spring bulb planting, 116
    storing, 82
    summer planting, 60
Buttercups, 80

Cabbage,
    cabbage/sprout, 4
    feeding, 105
    planting and spacing, 59
    winter harvesting time, 127
Cactus
    care, 157
    Christmas, 9
    Thanksgiving, 10
Calceolaria, annual, 67
Calendula, sowing, 58
Callicarpa japonica (beauty berry),
    134
Camellia,

air layering, 94
moving, 20
pruning, 48
winter protection, 125
Canary creeper, 67
Canterbury bells, transplanting, 108
Cape primrose, see Streptocarpus
Carrots,
    July sowing, 90
    Reemay cloth, 58
    sowing time, 58
    winter protection, 126
Caterpillars, 72
Cats,
    keeping off garden, 56
Cattails, 78
Cauliflowers,
    planting and spacing, 59
    summer sowing, 82
Cedar,
    hedge trimming, 97
    topping, 97
Celeriac,
    harvesting, 127
Celery,
    blanching, 127
    feeding, 105
    harvesting, 127
Chaenomeles,
    moving, 20
    pruning, 47
Charcoal, 6
Chard, for colour, 68
Chinese lanterns, see Physalis
Chives, 39
    for baskets, 53
Christmas door sprays and
    table centres, 154
Christmas trees, 153
Clarkia, 52
Clematis, layering, 94
Clivia, 10
Cloche, plastic,
    uses, 37
Cold frame,

cleanup, 112
construction, 55
use of, 23, 43, 52, 95
Compost, 128
building bins, 129
how to, 128
prefabricated bins, 130
seaweed, 130
temporary pile, 110
trench method, 130
Corn,
planting time, 56, 64
starting inside, 64
Cornus alba sibirica (red osier
dogwood), 143
Cornus stolonifera flaniramea (yellow
osier dogwood), 143
Corylus avellana contorta (Harry
Lauder's walking cane), 144
Cosmos, 67
Creeping charlie, see Pilea
Creeping fig,
in basket, 148
summer care, 85, 92
Creeping trefoil, see Weeds
Cress, curled,
how to grow, 127
Crocuses, 117
Crop rotation, 3, 110
Cucumbers,
on trellis, 65
planting time, 56
Curcubit family, 65
Currants, 14
Cutworms, 73
Cyclamen,
care, 156
houseplant, 9
Cymbidium, 10
summer care, 85

Daffodils,
aftercare, 59
in patio pots, 117

Dahlia,
dividing, 123
lifting and storing, 123
support staking, 61
tuber planting time, 60
Delphiniums, 50
Dandelion, see Weeds
Dibber, 43
Dieffenbachia, see Dumb cane
Digging,
spring, 21
winter, 136
Disabled Independent Gardeners
Association, 30
Diseases,
fungus, 3, 74
Dish gardens, 115
planting up, 115
selecting containers, 115
Dogwood
blotch, see disease, 74
possible control, 75
Dormant oil, 16
Dormant spraying, 16
Dracaena, stem cutting, 27
Drainage material, in patio pots, 62
Dumb cane (*Dieffenbachia*), stem
cuttings, 27

Eleagnus umbellata (autumn olive),
winter use, 144
Endive, winter crop, 127
English daisies, see Weeds
Epiphyllum (orchid cactus), summer
care, 85
Erica carnea, planting, 119
Euonymus alatus (winged
spindleberry), 133
Euonymus europeas (spindleberry),
144
Evergreens,
winter protection, 145
trimming, 96

Fall colour, 133
Fatsia, overwintering, 125, 146
Felicia amelloides (blue marguerite),
    colour, 67
Fertilizer,
    adding for planting, 68
    for hanging baskets, 81
    for lawns, 68
    for patio pots, 81
    for potting mix, 10
Figs, see also creeping fig,
    edible, 111
    protecting, 111
    ripening, 111
Firethorn, see *Pyracantha*
Fittonia (nerve plant), 6
Flowering maple, see *Abutilon*
Flowers,
    feeding, 105
    for cutting, 49
    preserving, 99
Foliage,
    preserving in glycerine, 100
Forsythia,
    moving, 20
    pruning, 47
Freckle plant, see Hypoestes
Freesia,
    'Paradise strain', 60
    planting time, 60
Fruit trees,
    planning, 44
    pruning, 138
    root stocks, 46
    selection and planting, 45
Fuchsia,
    flowering season, 108
    for baskets, 53
    overwintering, 124
    starting up, 22
    tree, 23
Fungicides, 74
Fungus diseases, 140

Garden,
    evaluation, 109
    maintenance, 81
    memberships, 153
    planning, 110
Gardenia, 12
    summer care, 85
Geraniums, see Pelargoniums
Gladioli,
    lifting and storing, 123
    planting time, 60
Gloriosa daisies, 67
Gooseberries, 14, 15
Goutweed, 80
Greenhouse, 112
    cleanup, 112
    heating, 113
    selection, 113
    siting, 113
    use of, 23, 52
Ground covers, 71
    Arctostaphylos, 71
    creeping thyme, 71
    Rubus, 71
Gypsophila, annual, 67

Hanging baskets, 53
    replanting, 23
    winter, 119
Harry Lauder's walking cane,
    see *Corylus avellana contorta*
Heather, winter, see *Erica carnea*
Heating cable, 28
Heavenly bamboo, see Nandina
Helenium,
    as cut flowers, 51
Helichrysum (strawflowers), 99
Heliotrope, 5
    colour, 67
Helxine (babies' tears), 6
Herbs, 38
    drying, 101
    from seed, 38
    in a strawberry pot, 39

in pots, 39
supplier, 38
under lights, 141
Hibiscus, 4
annual, 4
houseplant/pruning, 12,
outside for summer, 85
Hoeing, 79
Holly, pruning, 98
Houseplants
fall and winter care, 132
from cuttings, 26
grow-lights, 132
pruning/maintenance, 12
repotting, 9
suitable for terrariums, 6
summer care, 84, 92
washing, 132
watering, 132
Hoya, 9
Hyacinths,
aftercare bedding, 59
aftercare forcing, 12
for patio pots, 117
Hypericum calycinum (Rose of
Sharon), 119
Hypoestes (freckle plant), 28

Impatiens,
from seed, 34
New Guinea impatiens, 67
Iris,
flag, *Iris germanica*, 83
planting, 83
water, 78
Ivy, 148

Japanese quince, see Chaenomeles
Japonica, see Chaenomeles
Jasmine, 7
J. nudiflorum, 7
J. polyanthum, 9
Junipers, trimming, 97

Kalanchoe, 151
Kale, 82, 119
Kinikinik, see *Arctostaphylos*

Lantana, 85
Larkspur, 67, 51
Laurel hedge, trimming, 98
Lawns,
aeration, 70
feeding, 68, 105
top dressing, 70
weeds, 69
Layering, 94
Leeks, 108, 127
Lettuce,
as a summer crop, 89
as winter crop, 127
sowing spring, 58
winter lettuce, 142
Lime, 21
Lime sulphur, 16
winter wash, see Fungus
diseases,
Lobelia,
in hanging baskets, 53
seed sowing, 35
Loganberries, 15
Logbook, 2
Love-in-a-mist, see Nigella
Lupins, 50

Magnolia,
air layering, 94
pruning, 48
stellata, 48
Manure, 21, 137
Marguerite, blue, see *Felica
amelloides*
Marguerites,
overwintering, 124
planting time, 58
Marigolds,
for colour, 67

for patio pots, 62
marsh, 78
Matthiola, 5
Mechanical weeders, 80
Michaelmas daisy, see Aster
Mignonette, 5
Mildew,
    on apples, 75
    on begonias, 76
    on roses, 87
Mint, 39
Morning glory, see Weeds, 80
Moss,
    as a ground cover, 70
    hanging baskets, 53
    in lawns, 69
Mountain ash, 134
Mouse damage, 145
Mulch, 16, 22, 81

Nandina (heavenly bamboo), 125
Narcissi,
    paperwhites, 12
Nemesia, 4
Nerve plant, see Fittonia
New Guinea impatiens, see
    Impatiens
Nicotiana, 4, 67
Nigella (love-in-a-mist), 67
Nitrogen nodules, 3
Norfolk Island pine, 85

Onions, 126
Orange, miniature, 156
Orchids, cymbidium, 10

Pansies,
    sowing spring, 81
    winter, 82, 119
Parsley, for baskets, 53
Parsnips,
    feeding, 108

harvesting, 127
Parthenocissus heterophylla (Virginia
    creeper), 135
Patio gardens, 61
Patio planter,
    construction, 147
Pear trellis rust, 91
Peas, 3, 37
Pelargoniums (geraniums),
    cuttings, 103
    for baskets, 53
    overwintering, 124
    starting up after storing, 22
Peony, 32
Peperomia,
    in gift basket, 148
Peppers, 64, 66
Perennials,
    as cut flowers, 49
    cutting back, 111, 137
    dividing, 31
    moving, 20
    planting, 50
Periwinkle, 53
Pernettya mucronata, 134
Pesticide, 72, 73
Pests, 72
Petunia,
    for baskets, 53
    for patio pots, 62
    sowing, 34
Phacelia campanularia (California
    bluebell),
    colour, 67
Philodendron, 85
Physalis (Chinese lanterns),
    drying, 99
Pilea,
    aluminum plant, 28
    base cuttings, 28
    creeping charlie, 6
Pine tree,
    pruning, 97
Planning, 3
Plantain, see Weeds

Planting for colour, 66
Poinsettia,
    care, 156
    gift basket, 148
    how to make bloom, 123
Ponds, see Water gardens
Poppy,
    annual, 4
    California, colour, 67
    sowing, 58
Potatoes, 14
    grown in half-barrel, 63
    harvesting and storing, 126
    in tires, 64
    planting, 56
    varieties, 14
Potpourri, 87
    recipe, 101
Potting, 9
    houseplants, 10
    overwintered plants, 22
Primrose, see primula
Primulas,
    around ponds, 78
    sowing, 81
    transplanting, 108
Privet, hedge trimming, 98
Propagation,
    leaf, 26
    mix, 28
    shrub, 94
    stem, 27
    summer, 102
    tip, 28
Pruners,
    care, 140
    Felco, 150
Pruning saw,
    as gift, 151
    use, care and maintenance, 140
Pruning,
    berrybushes, 14
    fruit trees, 138
Prunus subhertella autumnalis, 8, 134
Pumpkin,

    how to plant, 65
Pyracantha (firethorn), 134
Pyrethrum daisy, 83

Radish, 58, 59
Ranunculus, planting, 118
Raised beds, 22
    construction, 29
Raspberries,
    fall bearing, 14
    planting, 45
    pruning, 14, 111
    rust disease, 75
    selection, 45
Reemay cloth, 58
Rhododendrons,
    deadheading, 49
    moving, 20
    pruning, 48
    siting, 19
Rhubarb chard, see Chard
Rhubarb,
    as pesticide, 73
    disease, 75
Rose of Sharon, see Hypericum
    calycinum
Roses,
    aphids, 86
    black spot, 87
    climbing, 25
    crown gall, 25
    fall pruning, 146
    mulching, 86
    multiflora, 25
    planting, 40
    polyantha, 25
    potpourri, 87
    powdery mildew, 87
    pruning hybrid teas, 24
    pruning rambler , 111
    rose care, 86
    winter mounding, 146
Rutabagas, 127

Sage, 39
  in a basket, 53
Salvia, 67
Seed,
  catalogues, 1
  saving, 102
  sowing, 34
  sowing too early, 21
  storing, 2
Seedlings, transplanting, 42
Selaginella (sweat moss), 6
Shrubs, 5
  cuttings, 94
  moving,5
  planting, 18
  pruning, 47
  winter flowering, 7
Slugs,
  control, 73
Snapdragons,
  longevity, 82
  planting, 58
  sowing, 34
Soil,
  sterilizing, 34
  terrarium mix, 6
Spinach, 58
Spindleberry, winged, see *Eonymus alatus*
Squash, 4
  planting, 64, 65
  spaghetti, 4
Stagshorn fern, 152
Statice,
  for drying, 99
Stewartia pseudocamellia, 84, 134
Stock,
  night scented, 5
  planting time, 58
Strawberry pot,
  in baskets, 53
  planting herbs in, 39
  selection/planting, 45
Strawflowers (helichrysum), 99
Streptocarpus,

cuttings, 27
Sweet pea,
  from seed, 51
  for cutting, 51
Swoe, 80

Tayberry, 15, 111
Terra Sorb, 52
Terrariums, 5
Thermometer, 152
Tibouchina,
  outside summer, 85
  overwintering, 124
Tomatoes, 3
  blossom end rot, 105
  late feeding, 105
  planting time, 56, 64
  ripening, 108
  seed sowing, 35
  staking and trimming, 88
  'Tiny Tim' for baskets, 53
  varieties, 3
Tools,
  as gifts, 152
  maintenance, 16
  terrarium, 5
Top dressing, see Mulch
Trees,
  moving, 5
  planting, 18
  pruning, 47, 138
  staking, 19
  winter staking, 145
Tulips, 59

Vegetables, 3
  brussels sprouts, 4
  feeding, 105
  harvesting and storing, 126
  peas, 3
  planting time, 57, 59, 63
  potatoes, 4
  seed saving, 102

spaghetti squash, 4
tomatoes, 3
zucchini, 4
Verbena, 67
Viburnum farreri, 8
Viola, white, 67
Virginia creeper, see *Parthenocissus heterophylla*

Wallflowers,
    sowing, 81
    transplanting, 108
Watering,
    computerized system, 30
    containers, 81
Water gardens, 77
Water lilies, 78
Weather,
    cool/wet, 90
    winter, 145
Weeds,
    clover, 69
    creeping trefoil, 69
    dandelion, 69
    English daisies, 69
    in lawn, 69
    perennial, 80
    plantain, 69
    weeding, 79
Weeping fig,

leaf loss, 92
Weevils,
    control, 72
Widger, 43
Winter cherry, see *Prunus subhertella autumnalis*, 8
Winter garden flowers, 7
Winter jasmine, see (*Jasminum nudiflorum*), 7
Winter planters, 118
Winter protection,
    styrofoam picnic coolers, 146
    wire and leaves, 111, 125
Wisteria,
    layering, 94
    pruning, 48
Wood preservative, 61

Yellow osier dogwood, see *Cornus stolonifera flaviramea*
Yew, hedge trimming, 98
Yucca, stem cuttings, 27

Zinnias,
    as cut flowers, 51
    for colour, 67
    from seed, 51
Zucchini, 65